Character First

Character First

The Hyde School Difference

Joseph W. Gauld

PRIMA PUBLISHING

© 1995 by Joseph W. Gauld

PRIMA PUBLISHING and colophon are trademarks of Prima Communications, Inc.

Library of Congress Cataloging-in-Publication Data

Gauld, Joseph W.
    Character first: the Hyde School difference / Joseph W. Gauld.
        p.   cm.
    Originally published: San Francisco: ICS Press, c1993.
    ISBN 0-7615-0160-6
    1. Hyde School (Bath, Me.). I. Title.
LD7501.B3475 1995
372.9741'85—dc20   95-21483
                                                CIP

95 96 97 98 99 DD 10 9 8 7 6 5 4 3 2 1
Printed in the United States of America

How to Order:
Single copies may be ordered from Prima Publishing, P.O. Box 1260BK, Rocklin, CA 95677; telephone (916) 632-4400. Quantity discounts are also available. On your letterhead, include information concerning the intended use of the books and the number of books you wish to purchase.

To my wife, Blanche, whose spirit continues to inspire the lives of everyone who knew her. She died as she lived: with courage, integrity, wisdom, and compassion.
Without her, Hyde School would not have been possible.

Contents

Preface

America's education system is a relic of a former age. It can't be reformed, resurrected, or restored. No amount of tinkering with the horse and buggy will produce an automobile. It's time for a new system.

I was raised on the notion that Americans don't talk about a problem, they go out and do something about it. So in 1966, after many years of teaching within a system I knew was fundamentally unsound, I quit, took a deserted mansion in Bath, Maine, and founded Hyde School. I was determined to explore a new educational premise that every youngster is gifted with a "unique potential" that defines a destiny—my interpretation of America's ideal that every individual is endowed with dignity and worth.

What emerged was a dynamic new philosophy of education, built on the foundation of unique potential, focused on character development, and centered on the family. Over the years, this philosophy has drawn out enormous potential from students—potential that was barely touched by their previous schools.

America thrives on bold, "break the mold" solutions to our problems, applied with a brash "damn the torpedoes" spirit. On the strength of a piece of paper called the Declaration of Independence, our forefathers rejected a society that had taken over 150 years to build. They embarked on a revolution that succeeded in the face of tremendous opposition, much of it from colonials themselves. Eleven years after declaring independence, these bold revolutionaries framed the Constitution of the United States of America—a document that has not only shaped the character and development of our own country but profoundly influenced the entire world.

This book outlines the beginnings of a second American revolution. It presents a distinctly *American* solution to our education problems, one forged in the bold, "can do" spirit on which our nation was founded.

The time is ripe for a revolution of America's education system. This book is meant to sound a call to arms.

Acknowledgments

Character First is the product of my life with hundreds of Hyde students, their parents, and their teachers. You will meet some of these people in this book. I salute their courage and dedication and thank those who allowed their stories to be shared.

I owe a profound debt of gratitude to my past and present family, who have helped me create and sustain the Hyde dream. I want especially to thank my mother and stepfather; my children and their spouses: Malcolm and Laura, Laurie and Paul, Gigi and Don; my brother, Tom, and his family; and my sister, Joan, for their love and support over the years.

Finally, I wish to thank Bob Hawkins and the staff of the Institute for Contemporary Studies for having the vision to publish the book; Jeannine Drew, my editor, for helping breathe new life into the manuscript; and Frances Murray, my secretary, for helping me build that manuscript over the past seventeen years.

Introduction

I love kids. I can't resist little ones. We often knowingly catch each other's eye, on an airplane or while standing in line. Hyde School parents who know my gruff exterior laugh when the chairman of our board of trustees calls me a pussycat, yet my grandchildren and other faculty brats figure it out.

But I have spent my life working with the bigger kids. I'm a risk taker who would love Wall Street—except I'm already playing in a game where the complexities, excitement, and stakes are truly in the big leagues. The assertion that the battle of Waterloo was won on the playing fields of Eton makes sense to me, because I can see by the lives of my former students—some now entering their sixties—how adolescence is a crucial practice period that can graphically foretell a lifetime.

My forty-two years of working with teenagers have given me a sense of omniscience about life—as though I'm standing on top of a high hill with a panoramic view, watching each of my students struggle with the obstacle course of adolescence and knowing in advance what the outcome will be, by the way each tackles the course.

Knowing how critical the obstacles are in preparing youngsters for life, I want to call out, "Don't try to go around that scary hurdle; it's there for a reason. Don't quit that rocky path; it's meant to be hard. Avoid taking that shortcut; there are none in life. Don't let yourself get discouraged; the great ones just keep putting one foot in front of the other. Trust the process; it will help you find your purpose in life."

When my students have the courage to face the obstacle course, I see them develop the self-confidence they will need to endure the adversities of life, and the self-understanding to find the path of their destiny. But when they try to avoid some of the obstacles or quit the practice field entirely, the results can be tragic. Then I helplessly watch as they wander aimlessly into adulthood or trudge down a well-worn, "safe" path that I know will offer them little fulfillment.

Unfortunately, society is blind to the reality that teens need to face and overcome difficult challenges if they are to become confident, productive, fulfilled adults. "Success" for adolescents in this society is measured, not by the number of challenges overcome, but by the number of *A*'s on their report cards. Good grades are the pipeline to a good college, which will lead to a good job (defined as one that pays lots of money), which supposedly leads to happiness ever after.

I have watched hundreds of teenagers pursue this road to "success." The bright ones found it an easy path and believed they had it made in life. I couldn't tell them they might wake up at forty to find themselves trapped in their "success," without a deeper sense of fulfillment. The kids who weren't as bright found the path difficult and often became unnecessarily discouraged, believing they were destined for lesser things. Both academic "haves" and "have nots" began to believe ability or luck were the keys to life. Teenage challenge and discovery slowly became lost arts.

To refocus education on the development of character and a deeper sense of purpose, I decided to found a boarding school to develop an obstacle course for *all* teenagers. Those who showed up on the doorstep of Hyde School were usually discouraged or screwing up badly enough to be willing to try something new. All we had to do was strip away their unproductive attitudes, challenge their character, and teach them to believe in themselves, and their lives would be set on a meaningful course. Or so I thought.

As I watched the first groups of Hyde graduates move on to college and then settle into their lives, I sensed that something was wrong. Our results were good, but still mixed. My instincts told me our obstacle course was missing something. The answer finally hit me like a ton of bricks: parents!

You probably think I'm pretty dense not to realize that parental attitude and involvement ultimately determine a kid's future. But for me the idea really was a curveball. When I founded Hyde School I thought I could reach *any* kid. But over time I couldn't help noticing that when we confronted students with important challenges, they would meet those challenges only if their parents' values and actions (not *words,* mind you) matched our teaching.

I felt dumb. Here I was, up on the hilltop, dispensing advice to kids as they struggled with the obstacle course, and thinking they were hanging on to my every word, when in fact what they did really depended upon their parents.

Eventually I figured it out: if I wanted to truly make a difference in the lives of kids, I had to make a difference in their parents. So in 1974 I founded the Hyde Family Learning Center to address parental growth and family issues. My hunch was right: the more we understood and dealt with the deeper struggles of Hyde parents and families through the Family Learning Center, the better Hyde students performed.

In time I came to realize that how parents had handled their own adolescence profoundly influenced their children's growth. Finally it all began to make sense: If we ourselves weren't guided through the obstacle course of adolescence, how could we guide our children? To help our children do better than we did, we must first learn to help ourselves better than we were helped. If we have the courage to examine our own lives and develop our own character, we will not only better ourselves, we will profoundly better our children's lives.

I began this introduction with an image of myself being

atop a high hill watching students struggle with adolescence, and pointing the way for them. But young people also give *me* direction. Hyde School creates a culture in which all participants—teachers and parents as well as kids—are students, learning from one another. At Hyde, wisdom is sought by everyone, not just dispensed by adults.

The educational philosophy outlined in these pages is a challenging one. Developing character and discovering unique potential are no simple tasks. Every successful Hyde participant develops a deep reverence for the maxim, The truth will set you free, but first it will make you miserable. The quest for one's destiny is never easy—or finished. But it is life's most rewarding journey despite the difficulties.

A word about how to read this book: On rare occasions we have all witnessed some individual—perhaps in music or sports—perform so spectacularly we describe him or her as "unconscious." Please try to read this book "unconsciously," as an experience. Don't restrict your deeper insights by rejecting what you currently disagree with or don't fully understand.

The Hyde philosophy cannot be adequately described in words; it must be *lived* to be fully comprehended. It's not uncommon to have a student call me five, ten, or even fifteen years after graduating to say, "Mr. Gauld, *now* I understand what you were trying to teach me!" It is my hope that you will have a similar reaction, that you will pick up this book from time to time and continue to gain new insights from it as a result of your own growth and development.

CHAPTER 1

Good-bye to the System

Sow an action, and you reap a habit.
Sow a habit, and you reap a character.
Sow a character, and you reap a destiny.
— Anonymous

When I was discharged from the navy I had no idea what I wanted to do next. My brother Tom had decided to go to college. True to our family values, he now became an admirably hard worker at prep school, making me follow suit. Through this late effort, and in spite of our hopeless high school records, he made Harvard and I got a summer school trial at Bowdoin.

I barely survived college. Then I got married and spent a year in sales, following my classmates' knee-jerk reflex of making a lot of money and becoming "successful." But try as I might, I knew my heart wasn't in it, and I slowly and reluctantly accepted the fact that I was destined to become a teacher. At the time this humiliated me. I felt I had dropped out of the race and would never be heard from again ("Those who can, do; those who can't, teach"). Today I am thankful I obeyed something deeper within me and followed my true calling.

Once I had made the choice to become a teacher, I found myself both motivated and confident. I dedicated myself to becoming a student of football, basketball, and baseball, and I earned my master's degree in math during summers at Boston University. I became head of the Math Department, director of athletics, director of admissions, and eventually assistant headmaster of New Hampton School, an independent school in New Hampshire. I eagerly sought each new assignment because to me, it wasn't a job, it was a part of my destiny.

But the more I achieved, the more concerned I became about the serious shortcomings of our educational system. Building a "better" school meant getting kids into "better" colleges so they could become "successful." No matter what we preached, character, attitude, and even effort were not the prime ingredients for success in school, and the kids knew it. Those with the right academic abilities were led to believe they had it made in life, while the kids without them were unnecessarily discouraged.

In my advanced placement calculus class, I was trying to tell a self-centered, apathetic fourteen-year-old genius that he was totally unprepared for life—while giving him my highest grade. On the other hand, I was trying to convince a totally discouraged Vermont farm boy that his character and

9

determination might someday make him the best engineer in the class—then assigning him my lowest grade.

Following up years later, I found that although the genius graduated from MIT at eighteen with an *A* average, he had long been unemployed. The disheartened farm boy, on the other hand, had become a top consulting engineer.

A Deeper Purpose

When I became director of admissions at New Hampton, I began to probe the vision and values of students in interviews. The goals of every candidate seemed the same:

"Why do you want to come here?" I asked.

"To get better grades . . ."

"Why?"

"To get into a better college . . ."

"Why?"

"To get a better job . . ."

"Why?"

"To make more money . . ."

"Why?"

"Uh . . . to . . . to . . . uh . . . be happy!" (this said while looking at me as if I had a screw loose)

When I hypothetically offered these candidates all the money they wanted, but with the stipulation they could not work, they became confused. This was often their first clue that the accepted definition of success—simply having a lot of money—might not ultimately satisfy them. When I could get candidates to search for the deeper purpose of their lives, it was both awe-inspiring and profound to note their almost universal expressions:

"To be the best I can be . . ."

"To help other people . . ."

"To leave the world a better place . . ."

Unfortunately, very little was being done, either at home or at school, to encourage these deeper visions. So I began to watch students go into life on the success treadmill, trusting that happiness was connected to keeping up with the Joneses. (Today I note the often ruinous consequences of this misguided concept of purpose as I interview young-sters of the next generation and find them generally bewil-dered by these questions, often resenting them as "too personal.")

Taking a Chance on Marty

To build a "better" school at New Hampton, we had to offer more sophisticated academic courses, which in turn required us to admit students with higher IQs. So I found myself accepting academically bright kids who often lacked a deeper sense of purpose, while having to turn down the students with average IQs who demonstrated character, drive, and determi-nation.

One day I finally rebelled. I was interviewing a wild-eyed kid named Marty,* with his policeman father. Marty was totally unqualified for our school: average IQ, flunking all his courses, and I heard he'd been in trouble with the police.

But I could feel his drive and desire and could sense his leadership potential. And every time I tried to let him down easy, I would get hypnotized by those damn eyes. I knew no one else was going to take this kid; what would happen to him if I didn't? What the hell was I in this business for? So I accepted Marty—and even talked the headmaster into offer-ing him a scholarship.

Marty was a fierce competitor and could so inspire others that he helped my teams win just about everything in sight. He also managed to break just about every rule in sight; he was enough trouble to make the faculty wonder whether I had compromised the school by admitting him.

I managed to help Marty get a college scholarship; he responded by getting tossed out his first term. I'd heard through the grapevine about his drinking and carousing and that the trim and fit athlete I'd known had ballooned to 250 pounds. The dean would hardly listen to my plea to keep the door open for Marty should he wish to return to college.

---

* Not his real name. In most cases the names of students have been changed for reasons of confidentiality.

Twice I wrote to Marty, asking him to visit me; there was no reply. I wrote again: "Just send a postcard to kiss me off like you have everyone else." He came.

Marty accepted my advice to take a service hitch. He joined the army, married a German woman, returned to the college that had expelled him, and graduated cum laude. Afterward, I helped him get a job in teaching. He eventually earned a Ph.D. in psychology and now operates a counseling service for parents, children, and families. Today he is also a member of the Hyde Board of Advisers.

Marty and I had a victory celebration some years ago. As we toasted his success, he made a comment that cuts to the core of what it means to be an effective teacher: "You believed in me when I didn't believe in myself."

Selling "Cracked Engine Blocks"

My experience with Marty reinforced my growing concern over the unfairness of the traditional educational system— what I have come to think of as just "the system." Kids like Marty were told in subtle and not so subtle ways that they couldn't hope to make much of themselves, while academically brighter students were given the false impression that their innate abilities ensured their success in life.

I didn't realize how deeply discouraged I was until the New Hampton faculty New Year's Eve party in 1962. I loved opportunities to get to know the personal side of the people I worked with. But as the evening developed I could sense that something was wrong. I felt a growing emptiness. My smile was fixed; I was trying too hard to be sociable.

Finally, I couldn't take it anymore; I had to go off by myself. I ended up sitting alone in the dark on the edge of a deserted stage, overlooking the basketball court. I could hear laughter and music below in the faculty lounge.

I cried for the first time in years, hardly understanding why. I was not drunk. I felt like a maudlin fool; I told myself I was being ridiculous. But for the life of me, I could not stop those tears.

At thirty-five, I had reached the top of my profession as a teacher, coach, and administrator. Now my appointment as assistant headmaster made it seem inevitable that soon I would become a headmaster of some prestigious prep school. I was approaching the pinnacle of success. But I lacked a deeper sense of fulfillment. I knew my conscience was confronting me.

On the same stage the month before, I'd played the role of Chris in the faculty production of Arthur Miller's *All My Sons*. In the play, Chris, a young idealist, returns from World War II and discovers that his father has knowingly shipped out cracked engine blocks, which resulted in the deaths of twenty-one American pilots. His father tries to explain that whatever he did was for his family, that he was desperately trying to save the business so he could leave it for his sons. But in the end Chris makes his father realize "they were all my sons." The father commits suicide.

Until this point, I'd always been able to limit my concern for kids to our own students; secretly I took satisfaction in the misfortunes of opposing teams or rival schools. But the play had reached something deep within me that told me I could never again draw such a line.

I'd realized I was part of an educational system that was selling "cracked engine blocks" to kids, whether they or anyone else would ever realize it. At first, I felt too insignificant and powerless to do anything about the situation. But, I reasoned, if it wasn't my responsibility to change the system, just *whose* responsibility was it?

I felt a cold shiver as I realized what *All My Sons* had taught me. Our educational system was failing kids everywhere, and I had to accept that they were *all* my responsibility. I was at the crossroads. The empty feeling in my stomach that night told me that no matter how successful I might appear, no matter how assured my future as a headmaster, I could not take that path.

I got up and walked back to the party. Now my empty feeling was replaced by a profound inner tension. I knew I had made a New Year's resolution that would ultimately change the entire course of my life.

The Birth of Hyde School

That summer I met with a Washington, D.C., group that included Robert Kennedy to explore the possibility of founding a new school. The effort ended when John Kennedy was assassinated, but it put me into motion. In 1964 I accepted the headmastership of Berwick Academy in South Berwick, Maine, and introduced a program that emphasized building character and developing the unique potential of each student. I projected a dynamic role with new responsibilities for students, which in turn placed new demands on the faculty to work with students at a deeper level. I worked hard to create an energetic atmosphere of continual change for all.

While I was encouraged by the new spirit my efforts brought to the school, I soon found myself embroiled in conflicts with the trustees, who were not yet ready to accept the sweeping changes I was proposing. Rather than compromise the program, I finally resigned after a year.

I was proud of the way I had stood by my principles, but I was totally at sea as to what to do next. Another headmastership seemed fruitless, because my experience at Berwick confirmed I was envisioning change beyond what the system could or would absorb. But attempting to found a new school without resources or experience, combined with my leadership failure at Berwick, seemed foolhardy. If I failed, how would I provide for my family?

But despite my fears, I could not ignore the powerful inner voice reminding me of the New Year's Eve commitment I'd made in 1962. So in 1965 I set out with a "California or bust" commitment to found a school. Thanks to loans from my three brothers and Sumner Hawley, my closest friend and associate at New Hampton; donations from the three heirs of the Hyde family; and the help of others, our new board of trustees was able to purchase the Hyde Estate in Bath, Maine.

The estate contained an elegant brick Georgian mansion, surrounded by 145 wooded acres. It had been the home of John S. Hyde, a member of the family that founded the Bath Iron Works and developed it into one of the major shipbuilding centers in the United States. The mansion was erected in 1913 by John Hyde's employees. With no ships to build at the time,

Hyde had thus found a way to keep his skilled employees on the payroll. The house was built like a ship, too, with huge steel girders providing the main supports.

The Hyde family had vacated the estate in the 1940s and had made it available to the Pine Tree Society for Crippled Children and Adults, which used it as a center for polio victims in the 1950s and 1960s, until the development of the Salk vaccine rendered the facility obsolete. We purchased the estate in January of 1966 and renamed it Hyde School.

It seemed amazing to the faculty, my wife, and me that an entire school could be housed in a mansion originally designed for one family. In the fall we would board fifty-four students and faculty members in the remodeled third-floor ballroom and in the bedrooms, servants' quarters, and carriage house. The school would not outgrow the mansion's massive dining room and kitchen until enrollment reached one hundred fifty students!

A speech and hearing center previously built onto the mansion provided ample classrooms and office space. Several faculty families could be housed on the estate, and the front yard was large enough to serve as a football practice field. Kids who wanted more exercise could take an elevator to the swimming pool in the basement.

The spring of 1966 was filled with frantic activity: a search for students, teachers, and staff; the renovation of our new facilities; and the purchase of everything from desks to football uniforms. My wife, Blanche, our three children, Audrey (my secretary, who also helped with the kids), and I set up an assembly line in the living room, sorting and stuffing brochures to be mailed to guidance counselors throughout the eastern United States.

I knew that faculty selection would be crucial to the successful development of our new concept. Teaching is a challenging profession, but the demands on Hyde teachers would be far greater than those at a traditional school; Hyde faculty would have to help pioneer a new concept of education and inspire students to entrust their futures to our as yet unproven vision. I wanted teachers who were deeply committed to growing children and enthusiastic about being part of the Hyde experiment. I also expected their academic competence to guide the school's transition from an emphasis on academics to an emphasis on character.

I thought it would be easy to find experienced teachers frustrated enough to jump at the opportunity of teaching at Hyde, so I was very surprised at the hesitancy I encountered. Even Sumner Hawley, who had shared my vision for a better way of education when we taught together at New Hampton, balked initially. But Sumner did come aboard, and he was joined by several others who were disillusioned with the system and had the courage to participate in our grand experiment.

Hyde School opened on June 28, 1966, three days before we signed the papers making our purchase of the Hyde Estate official. Forty-one boys, in grades nine through twelve, were admitted to the summer session (Hyde didn't become coed until 1971).

The night before the first day of classes, Blanche and I, our children, faculty members, and workmen strolled from room to room inspecting our renovation of the stately Hyde Mansion, glistening in all of its restored grandeur. As I marveled at the beautiful workmanship, I envisioned the students who would learn and grow in these majestic surroundings. I knew that my long odyssey through the system was over. Whatever my future, I would at least be honoring my deeper instincts.

The Hyde Philosophy

From its inception, Hyde School was bent on creating a unique learning atmosphere, one that valued the need for students to search for a sense of purpose and destiny that could be attained by bringing out the best in themselves by discovering their unique potential. A person's unique potential is akin to an inner calling and reflects his or her temperament, gifts, natural talents, dreams, aspirations, background, and traditions. It is the person waiting to be born in each of us out of our own unique amalgamation of background and experiences.

The concept of unique potential is not new; it can be traced

back at least as far as the early Greeks. The Greeks believed that each of us has a *daimon,* or perfect self, within us and that living up to that inner self, or unique potential, is the destiny of each individual. Thus the Greek philosophy of education could be reduced to two simple credos: Know thyself, and Become what you are.

I was determined that our founding principle—Every individual is gifted with unique potential—would guide the school. I had seen what getting kids into the "right" colleges or maintaining a school's public image could do to destroy true uniqueness. School loyalty or pleasing parents, teachers, or trustees would not be allowed to compromise the growth of students at Hyde. I would require regular evaluations of the personal and academic growth of each student, and I would make every teacher a guidance counselor to help ensure our focus on unique potential.

Hyde's underlying philosophy makes it radically different from the traditional American high school, as can be seen in

	Present educational system	Hyde School
Key concept	Academic knowledge	Unique potential
Basic foundation	Inborn academic ability	Character
Key student resources	Intellect, wealth	Conscience, hard work
Ultimate goal	College, material success	Life
Standard of excellence	Academic achievement	Growth, character development
Key teacher resource	Knowledge, academic background	Commitment to student growth
Primary overseers	So-called experts	Parents
Peer influence	Uncontrolled	Focused on shared responsibility

the chart contrasting Hyde School and the system. Whereas the traditional school dispenses intellectual knowledge, Hyde pursues a deeper, more powerful agenda—developing the unique potential of students.

Because character, not IQ, is the foundation of unique potential, Hyde is not focused on students' innate intellectual abilities, which in any event are beyond their control. Instead of relying on intellect to produce good grades and high test scores, students at Hyde learn to follow the dictates of their conscience so they can develop the character necessary to bring out their unique potential.

If you wish to succeed in the system, your chances will be improved significantly if your family is wealthy. But for students to succeed in life—the ultimate goal of a Hyde education—wealth is not a requirement. (In fact, it can be a severe hindrance, as I have seen with dozens of students who came from wealthy families and who utterly failed to develop meaningful lives, or in some cases even to hold down a paying job.) All that is required to succeed at Hyde and beyond is the willingness to work hard.

Whereas the system at best prepares students for acceptance to college, Hyde School prepares them to lead responsible, meaningful, self-governing lives. We gauge our success in terms of students' character growth rather than their academic achievement, the traditional standard of excellence.

Although Hyde looks for academic competence in selecting faculty, we are equally concerned with a prospective teacher's willingness to commit to aiding the character growth of students. But while we expect their commitment, we don't view teachers or any other "experts" as having primary responsibility for overseeing the growth and development of Hyde students; that responsibility is reserved for parents. We have found time and again that committed parents are the primary factor in determining the level of success (that is, growth) that our students ultimately achieve in life.

Unlike schools in the system, Hyde requires that students take responsibility for one another and assist one another in developing their unique potential. Under the principle of Brother's Keeper, which we'll cover in a later section, students must ensure that their peers abide by Hyde's Five Principles and our code of ethics.

Courage, Integrity, Concern, Curiosity, Leadership

One might suspect, in analyzing the chart on page 18, that the Hyde philosophy trades academics for character. In fact, we have discovered that character excellence is the foundation of and the means to achieve academic excellence. Conversely, academic development is an integral part of character development; you don't get one without the other.

By "character," I mean those qualities that help individuals develop their unique potential. The central virtues of character are defined in the Hyde motto: Courage, Integrity, Concern, Curiosity, and Leadership. These have come to be known as the Five Words. Hyde expects all students to develop these traits:

- the *courage* to accept challenges
- the *integrity* to be truly themselves
- *concern* for others
- the *curiosity* to explore life and learning
- *leadership* in making the school and community work

The Five Words define the basic objectives of the character–unique potential curriculum at Hyde. They form the basis
for evaluating our programs and procedures. They are the
yardstick by which we measure our success; if we are being
effective, then we should be able to note the development of
these five qualities in our students.

A New Approach to Character-based Education

Whether and how to teach character in the classroom have
been major topics of concern throughout America's educational history. Efforts to set the proper standards of good
character in American schools have led to cries of "indoctrination" or studies that indicate such efforts produce only
superficial results, not true character development. On the
other hand, attempts to allow individuals to define character
on their own terms—such as the "values clarification" movement of the 1970s—have proved no better than indoctrination
in producing decent human beings or improving the character
of American society as a whole.

At Hyde we have discovered a way of addressing character
that avoids the opposite extremes of indoctrination and "doing your own thing." Although we teach certain values, we
don't attempt to indoctrinate students. Because we respect
unique potential, we believe that each student must ultimately
answer to his or her own conscience. This doesn't mean that
"anything goes." Hyde students also believe in unique potential. They have voluntarily committed to finding the best in
themselves, and they soon find that this commitment is
incompatible with "doing your own thing."

My own perception of character, on which the Hyde

curriculum is based, is that it includes an *inner* as well as an *outer* component. The outer component consists of those admirable traits, such as courage, integrity, concern, curiosity, and leadership, that others can observe in an individual and from which others can benefit.

By practicing these outward expressions of character, the individual develops his or her inner character—the foundation of unique potential. This unique potential, in turn, shapes the individual's outer expressions of character: one person may exhibit integrity by protesting what he sees as an unjust war; another may demonstrate equal integrity by serving in the same war, in which he firmly believes. Both are demonstrating the qualities of character, but their *interpretations* of these qualities differ.

Our dualistic concept of character forces teachers and students at Hyde to develop a workable bond because, according to our definition, the perception of either group alone is insufficient to define character. For example, a teacher might place a high value on respect for adults—an outer expression of character. But a student who appears outwardly disrespectful might in fact be demonstrating character by placing another legitimate value, such as truth or justice, above respect for authority. (This was true of many students who protested the Vietnam War and thus showed "disrespect" for authority.)

This teacher-student partnership confronts unproductive attitudes on both sides. Teachers find they cannot ignore the overall needs of students or rely upon authority alone to do their jobs, and students must confront the hypocrisy of keeping one foot in Hyde and one foot in a youth culture that encourages drug use and thus hinders the discovery of their unique potential. This approach is a far more compelling one than "Just say no"; it speaks to the deeper longing, expressed in student interviews, to "be the best person I can be."

The Learning Triangle

Hyde's focus on unique potential results in a radical shift in the traditional relationship between student, teacher, and

subject. Picture learning as a triangle with sides connecting the three vertices of teacher, student, and subject. Traditional education is built on the base of teacher and subject, who determine the third vertex, the student (see the learning triangle diagrams). So, in essence, the teacher and the subject mold the student.

But under the character–unique potential concept, teacher and student become the base, thus defining the third vertex, the subject. The overall objective of the Hyde program is to develop each student's unique potential rather than to make sure that students absorb a particular set of facts and learn a particular set of skills. Therefore, instead of the student being molded by the teacher and the subject, teacher and student use the subject as a tool to further the development of the student's unique potential.

This approach motivates students at a deep level, because it transforms education into something that is meaningful to

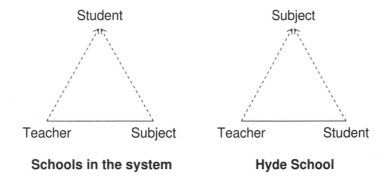

Student	Subject
Teacher Subject	Teacher Student
Schools in the system	**Hyde School**

them. When academic achievement becomes a means of realizing their dreams, of developing their full potential, students become serious, even passionate, about learning.

The Five Guiding Principles

Hyde's focus on character and unique potential overthrows the tyranny of test scores and grades, because it makes *growth* rather than *academic achievement* the measure of success. But this liberation also sacrifices the supposed objectivity of test scores and tends to leave us at the mercy of subjective human perceptions to evaluate the growth of our students and the success of our program.

What would prevent our character-based measurements from being unduly influenced by a student's popularity, or by the strong opinions of a particular teacher? What would provide our checks and balances, as the Constitution did on the president and his men during Watergate? We had to be certain that the overall process was guided by our basic principles, not by our strongest individuals.

I founded Hyde with no preconceived ideas as to how the character–unique potential concept might work. I believed if we truly committed ourselves, the idea itself would teach us how to put it into action. Over the years, we've found that Five Principles—Destiny, Humility, Conscience, Truth, and Brother's Keeper—have guided Hyde's growth and development.

Principle Number 1: Destiny

Each of us is gifted with a unique potential that defines a destiny.

The Hyde philosophy is based on this fundamental premise. The sole purpose of the Hyde program is to help each student find and develop his or her unique potential. In order to do so, parents and teachers must work on developing their own unique potential, because we cannot teach what we do not know.

The first responsibility of all Hyde participants is to learn to respect the unique potential of themselves and all other members of the community. Prejudices or personal biases are not acceptable in a unique-potential community; failing to fully appreciate another's value means failing to fully realize one's own.

I grew up in a racially segregated suburb of Washington, D.C., never realizing my own racial bias. When I finally recognized it, I made a special effort to develop friendships with black Americans, which helped bring out a part of me that many whites never tap. Prejudice is sometimes more destructive to the offender than to the offended.

Prejudices we maintain against ourselves can be even more destructive than those we hold against others. We may spend our lives wishing for what we don't have, or trying to become something we are not, and never learn to appreciate our own untapped potential. For example, my narrow-minded definition of success left me, as a young man, with a need to overcome my humiliation of ending up as a teacher. For a time, I was blocking my own destiny by seeing only a limited view of what it means to be a teacher.

We all harbor negative feelings about ourselves and our potential, but adolescents are particularly vulnerable to this tendency. This country should be deeply disturbed by the depth of shame that American youngsters are currently carrying into adult life as a result of trying to measure up to idealized media images and conform to unrealistic expectations set by parents, teachers, and peers.

It is remarkable to observe how deeply inhibited most students are when they first arrive at Hyde. During our summer orientation session, students are asked to sing a solo in front of their classmates, to participate in physical challenges, and to show their true selves to others in a variety of other ways. This is extraordinarily difficult for most of them, because they have been taught to feel deficient if they do not excel in every aspect of their lives, or if they don't conform to others' ideals and expectations.

It is vital that we help youngsters to overcome these inhibitions, examine themselves honestly and confidently, and learn to appreciate their own uniqueness. Otherwise, they can never hope to fulfill their destinies.

Principle Number 2: Humility

We trust in a power and purpose beyond ourselves.

At a primary level, we all need humility if we are to accept criticisms and suggestions and if we are to be able to admit to and grow from our mistakes. At a higher level, if we believe in the concept of destiny, by definition we also recognize there is a power and purpose beyond ourselves; this recognition gives birth to humility.

Unfortunately, these days humility is at the bottom of America's list of values. I've heard more than one American remark with disdain that "humility is for losers"! The problem for many of us is our belief in the rugged individual as some sort of Rambo who not only champions justice but does it single-handedly. This attitude undermines the development of unique potential by denying the very real human need to get help from others.

The power of humility can be witnessed in the extraordinary success record of Alcoholics Anonymous. The proliferation of twelve-step programs modeled on AA has been criticized lately because of their emphasis on giving over control to a "higher power." Perhaps some of the programs do go too far in this direction; we are, after all, ultimately responsible for our own lives. But the real strength of such programs lies in their acknowledgment that sometimes we need to go outside ourselves for help—a tough notion for individualistic Americans to accept. Our lives could improve dramatically if we learned to live by the serenity prayer:

God grant me the serenity *to accept the things I cannot change,*
The courage *to change the things I can,*
And the wisdom *to know the difference.*

We don't have to share a belief in God in order to practice the principle of humility. We need only to accept that none of us is the center of the universe. This is particularly important for parents, who must free their children to find their own destiny.

Although a belief in God is not a requirement for practicing humility, believing in a higher power may make it easier. But we must avoid indoctrinating others to our own perception of a higher power. Realizing unique potential requires a unique search for one's higher power and purpose. Promoting our beliefs, even with the best intentions, may actually divert others from finding their own faith.

I was thirty-five before I realized I actually believed in God and prayer in the way espoused by so many other people. Resisting what I perceived as indoctrination had actually turned me away from my own true beliefs! Faith is something we must ultimately discover for ourselves.

My experience at Hyde convinces me that the unique-potential process will inevitably lead students to explore the principle of humility. When I first founded Hyde, I required all students to attend religious services somewhere. I discontinued this practice when I realized it was turning students off. But at my optional Friday night meetings, students often wanted to talk about the meaning of life and God. Apparently our job is simply to help students find their best and trust a higher power to take care of the rest.

Principle Number 3: Conscience

We achieve our best through character and conscience.

Our major task in life is to develop the inner capacity to listen and effectively respond to the dictates of conscience, the compass that points us in the direction of our destiny. Once we help students to begin striving to achieve their best through the development of character, their true best will be inspired by their own consciences. The ultimate measure of our teaching success is not how well our students learn to listen to us but how well they learn to listen to the best in themselves, how well prepared they are to govern their own lives.

Our present system teaches to the student's ego, rewarding "right" actions and punishing "wrong" ones. Although this approach is acceptable, and even necessary, at the primary level, it is wrong for more advanced education, when students should be learning to listen to the voices of their consciences.

The ego's instincts are tuned to our emotions; ego feels success, failure, pleasure, fear, doubt, confidence, and so on. Without the guidance of conscience, ego will inflate excessively with success or deflate excessively with failure, get sidetracked easily, and avoid paths it fears or deems too difficult, thus making unique potential all the harder to discover and develop. It is clear that our teaching must help students transcend short-term ego gratification and trust the long-term promise of their inner compasses.

This principle of conscience has the power to inspire a higher plane of learning and teaching in our schools. As this concept is increasingly understood by a school-community, the group conscience becomes a tremendous resource for helping each individual sort out ego drives and become sensitized to a higher order of thought.

Principle Number 4: Truth

Truth is our primary guide.

Truth is the cement that holds together the foundation of the character–unique potential community. Individuals may disagree over the nature of a higher power or argue the priority of certain values, but we all accept truth as life's ultimate guide. Our beliefs may or may not be correct, but the truth is the truth, whether we believe it or not. Accepting truth as "a greater power" bonds the community.

Although truth is one of the foundations of Hyde School, it is not our only value. Blurting out the truth in every situation shows little judgment or discrimination. We must rely on conscience to dictate what to say or not to say in a given situation. A good rule of thumb is, When in doubt, bet on the truth.

The greatest gift we can give our children is the truth. If we suffer from some dark secret, then our children will suffer as well. Not knowing the truth has led many people to think the worst of themselves or their families; only the truth can set them free.

As parents and teachers, we will inevitably misperceive the truth at times; we all make mistakes. But giving children our best perception of the truth expresses our love and concern and allows them to trust us at the deepest level.

Hyde has identified five steps an individual must take to make a serious commitment to truth:

1.   Recognize the value of being honest with oneself.
2.   Realize that sustaining a trusting relationship with others requires one to be honest with others as well.
3.   Begin to share one's strengths, weakness, vision, and emotionally charged experiences with others.
4.   Use journaling to get in touch with true feelings and the deeper inclinations of the heart.
5.   Let go of images that keep one from being genuine.

Principle Number 5: Brother's Keeper

We help others achieve their best.

My Hyde experience has convinced me that we all have a natural instinct to help others, the expression of which develops our own unique potential. The Hyde process of character and unique potential takes the notion of helping others one step farther: making students accountable for helping one another achieve their best.

Today's morality has each of us traveling around in a bubble of "rights" that we expect others to respect—as long as it doesn't interfere with their bubbles. Concern in our society means, "Help me do what *I* want to do. If I am feeling bad, you are supposed to sympathize; it is improper to suggest I may be feeling sorry for myself." If some spoiled brat acts up at the supermarket, it would be considered shocking to suggest the mother try more discipline.

We may construe this bubble idea as freedom, but in reality it isolates us from one another. In Hyde's character–unique potential community we operate instead like a big family. We respect unique potential but not necessarily what is being done with it or an attitude that is being held, and we may say or act accordingly.

The Brother's Keeper concept dictates that I say or do what I truly believe is in your best interests, regardless of how it may make you feel about me. In my last year in college I half-jokingly suggested to my grandfather that I might come to work in his mill, teasing him that "I'd need an office," and other perks. He looked me square in the eyes and said, "No, you'd be no good at it." I laughed; he didn't. I felt humiliated and exposed for the playboy I was, trying to ride his coattails. But with time I realized how similar expressions of his deeper concern for me had helped guide me to my destiny.

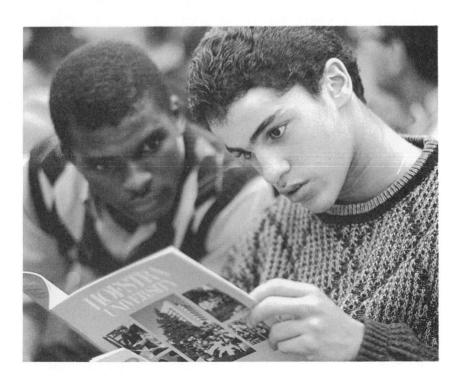

New Hyde parents in particular sometimes feel that Brother's Keeper makes the school's teachers and students insensitive, egotistical, or hurtful; their "personal rights" morality makes them hear our frank concern as criticism. Their egos haven't experienced a community truly committed to developing the best in themselves and their children.

Of course, the Brother's Keeper concept is sometimes overdone and *can* become insensitive and even interfering. But we have come to trust the community conscience to deal with such excesses.

Practicing the Five Words and Five Principles is the primary means of internalizing and growing from the concept of character–unique potential. Living by these guidelines, although tough and demanding, is ultimately energizing and rewarding. It has resulted in a richer, more rewarding and meaningful life for the entire Hyde community—and has led to academic excellence as well. The Hyde program prepares every student for college. In actual practice, 97 percent of Hyde graduates choose to attend four-year colleges, and more than 80 percent of those graduate within four years. Yet Hyde does not screen candidates on the basis of grades, IQ, or any other academic criteria. When you put character first, academic achievement naturally follows.

CHAPTER 2

The Hyde
Philosophy
in Action

Any student who's ever gone there ends up feeling strongly about it one way or the other. Hyde cuts very deep.

—a Hyde graduate

P aul Hurd, a senior in the local high school in Bath, was the first student admitted to Hyde in 1966. He arrived on our doorstep after having been rejected by three competitive colleges and assured by his guidance counselor that he would never achieve beyond an average level. He writes:

> In my own mind, I graduated from high school a flat failure. I had been shot down at all three of my college choices. I couldn't believe it. I thought I had done all the right things: maintained a *B+* average for three years, been active in student government, joined a variety of clubs, represented my high school at Boys State, and lettered in three varsity sports. Where had I gone wrong?

Part of the answer was a pair of mediocre scores on his College Boards. But Paul hints at another reason:

> In late January, the school guidance counselor called me in to express his distress: "Paul, you are simply applying way over your head. None of these colleges will give serious consideration to your scores. . . . Frankly, Paul, we cannot give strong support and recommendation to your present applications."
>
> I began to perceive the real problem: How could any college think I was worth taking a chance on against the damning evidence that my own high school wouldn't express pride or strong conviction about my accomplishments or about me?

Paul's parents weren't wealthy, but they were committed to the best education possible for their son. They, too, were stunned and confused that Paul, after a seemingly successful high school career, was unable to win a spot at a top-notch college.

As graduation neared, the family had to decide what to do next. Paul's father, a tireless optimist, came home one day in May with information about prep schools that offered post-graduate programs for students like Paul who needed an extra year of preparation to make themselves more attractive college candidates. Within a week, Paul began a round of interviews. One of the schools put him on a waiting list, but the headmaster recommended that Paul consider a new private school called Hyde, which was about to open in his hometown. He and his father soon arrived at my office for an interview.

The Admissions Interview

The Hyde concept of unique potential requires us to assume that every student is capable of excellence, given the right attitude, effort, and support. So we need to admit students not on their past records but on what they are ready and willing to do. A vigorous, in-depth interview has become almost our only criterion for admission.

The interview had little to do with academics but everything to do with whether a student and his family were ready and willing to face themselves and one another to pursue life at a deeper level. To determine if candidates could take an honest look at themselves, we would probe their attitudes toward themselves, family members, school, teachers, friends, and life in general. How did they view their own characters, strengths, and weaknesses? Did they know what they wanted out of life? If not, did they believe we could help them discover it? Could we reach their deeper feelings during the interview? How did they handle it when we did? The interview became a powerful learning experience that revealed how each candidate would ultimately react at Hyde.

We knew we had to explore parental attitudes and beliefs to determine whether we had a potential partnership with the family. For this reason, we had parents observe the entire interviewing process. (In later years we would interview parents as well and would discover that parents are the single most important factor in determining the ultimate success or failure of our efforts at Hyde.) Their reactions revealed our common ground and areas of disagreement that needed to be explored. The understanding and concern we showed during the interview helped parents to trust us later when the going got tough—which it often did.

Paul's Interview

Paul describes our interview:

> When we settled into soft chairs on the sun porch, I leaned back in expectation of another detached, casual chat about college. After several quick questions about family and success in school, Mr. Gauld dropped a bomb.
>
> "Why do you want to go to college?"
>
> At first I thought he was kidding. Doesn't everybody want to? Nobody had ever asked me that question, least of all myself. I was panicked.
>
> "To be able to get a better job," I ventured.
>
> "Is that the most important thing to you?"
>
> "Well, no, it's not exactly the most important . . ."
>
> "Well, what kinds of things do you want out of your life?"
>
> I was beginning to feel rattled. I glanced at my father and was struck by his intentness. After my detached interviews at other schools, spent talking about the weather, grades, and Board scores, these questions swept me off balance and left me at sea.
>
> However, Joe bailed me out of my embarrassment, commenting: "Those are probably questions you should be considering more and more at the age of seventeen." I thought I noticed my father nod.
>
> Later, I asked a few limp questions about courses and sports and felt as though I were asking an architect how screws and washers fit together . . .

Paul's parents were obviously dedicated to helping their son discover the best in himself, and our interview clearly revealed Paul's desire to succeed. But it also pointed to a deeper lack of self-confidence. Paul had met his school's academic standards, had been active in school life, and had become a "nice" kid, but deep down was left unchallenged. By his own admission, he had not lived up to his potential in high school: "I felt that very few of my high school performances characterized my best shot; at times I was guilty of sheer laziness."

I felt sure that Paul's lack of self-confidence had come through in his college interviews and had contributed to his rejections. In the absence of high test scores, there was nothing to distinguish him from the hundreds of other "nice kids" who were competing for admission. Much to his surprise, I told Paul I thought he'd be a good candidate for Hyde. His father remarked to his son, "We have a lot to think about."

The following week, Paul's mother visited with me. She went home that evening "ruffled but impressed," remarking to Paul, "He has a little nerve after one interview telling me there are a lot of things you need to face, but he also said that he couldn't imagine you being unable to handle the work at *any* college."

"From then on," Paul writes, "there was little question where I would take my postgraduate year, even when I was later accepted at one of my earlier choices."

A Test of Character

For a while, things went smoothly for Paul at Hyde. By the end of the first month, he was voted class president, had become a two-way starter in football, and was recognized as a serious student. Writing about those early days, he recalls that he was "floating along in a bubble of complacency." But the bubble soon burst as Paul met with his first test of character.

Another student asked Paul for copies of the French homework he'd missed due to a week-long illness; Paul complied. He recalls: "I didn't see any harm in helping him get caught up, and I was eager for his approval. He and several others had been outspoken in their criticism of my faculty relationships, and their criticism needled me. 'Sellout' was a title I couldn't stomach."

Before long other students approached Paul about "help" with their French homework. Paul gave in once again, rationalizing, "It's only homework. If they copy it, that's their problem, not mine. And besides, I'm only trying to help." Soon he was regularly circulating homework to about half the class. Although he had hoped to gain their friendship by doing so, he noticed that he "seemed to be losing instead of gaining their confidence and, more important, their respect. I felt used."

In mid-January a classmate, applying the Brother's Keeper principle, turned Paul in. Paul was furious:

> I felt betrayed, and profound resentment at what seemed to be a conspiracy to set me up and ruin a perfect year. I was in a rage. How could people do this to me? How could I have wound up in this spot with such good intentions? I wasn't a cheater!
>
> But the seriousness of Mr. Gauld's manner soon scared me past anger. I quickly admitted I'd been lending my homework to a few people to help them out. But if cheating was going on, I maintained, it was the fault of those borrowing, not mine.
>
> He hit the roof and I wanted to run: "Do you really feel they can cheat without your compliance? Is this the kind of leadership you feel your class and the school need? People put their faith in you to help set some direction, and how have you respected that?
>
> "Consider the injustice done to your classmates. They may gain the grade, but because only you did the work, only you have truly learned. So while you progress, they fall further behind."
>
> I felt that he just didn't understand the whole situation. I had been losing my classmates' confidence and wanted them to understand I cared. But when I told him this, somehow it didn't feel quite right.
>
> "Are you trying to be a leader or trying to be popular? There's a big difference. One requires courage, the other just a good sense of smell."
>
> Courage—so this was what we were really talking about. I felt stupid. Someone was holding a mirror in front of me and the reflection showed a pretty fair coward.
>
> I just sat there, stunned. Finally, Mr. Gauld broke

the silence: "You see, Paul, you are the worst culprit in this situation. If you had simply said no, no one would have been compromised. Don't try to duck what is your absolute responsibility."

This incident confirmed to Paul that Hyde "obviously meant business on a deeper level than I had been ready to deal with." The experience made a profound impression on him. From this point on he began to trust in himself on a deeper level and to follow his own inner direction rather than following the crowd.

Like most of his peers, Paul had tried to get into a top college in order to "get a better job." Now he began to examine himself and his values more deeply: "Strangely enough, I became so preoccupied with setting things right at school that my interest in college admissions cooled. I even considered that Bowdoin, the college I had earlier set my heart on, might not be the right place for me, something no one could have convinced me of the year before."

After his year at Hyde, Paul did reapply for admission to Bowdoin. While his College Board scores were only marginally better this time, in his admissions interview he clearly distinguished himself as being a confident young man who knew himself and what he wanted out of life. He was accepted at Bowdoin.

Applying the Brother's Keeper Principle

To be turned in by another student for cheating would have been unthinkable in Paul's previous school. But at Hyde, the principle of Brother's Keeper requires students to hold one another accountable for achieving their best.

Brother's Keeper is one of the hardest principles for incoming students to accept. The larger society's "rights" morality allows kids to hide behind the I-don't-rat-on-my-buddies ethic, which simply masks their fear of responsibility toward and deeper involvement with one another, as well as their doubts that such idealism can actually work. Students will readily maintain standards when given a specific role like

that of a proctor, but they feel any deeper show of specific concern for others would be resented and rejected.

But I know that kids will eventually respect a real stand on principles and beliefs. In the early days of Hyde I had endlessly explained why I prohibited smoking—but with limited success. Nevertheless, in time the kids slowly accepted and even respected my stand against the cigarette industry's exploitation of youth. So I clung to the Brother's Keeper concept and slowly made converts. When enough kids internalize such a concept, it is almost magical how they help new students to accept the concept virtually overnight.

Helen and Laura: A Lesson in Trust

Helen was a bright and attractive girl from a moneyed family, but she was raised in a virtual moral vacuum. She ended up in a fast-moving clique where hedonism was so rampant that

sex was being exchanged for drugs. And she was untrust-
worthy; stealing and lying had become a way of life for her.

When she arrived at Hyde, her lack of character was soon
confronted by another student. Helen remembers:

> I'd had a very tough summer, been on a work crew
> to deal with my attitude, and came to the regular year
> scared to death. In my mind no one trusted me.
>
> When I started to unpack, my roommate, Laura,
> didn't seem as intimidating as I had been hearing, but
> I felt very shy and wished I had a roommate I knew,
> one who wasn't thought of quite so highly in school.
>
> But Laura was very friendly and didn't launch into a
> speech on Hyde. As the term went on I began to feel
> more at ease with her. We laughed and joked together,
> and though at times it felt superficial, I felt there was
> a real understanding between us.
>
> Then one day a girl recognized her bracelet, which
> I'd taken during summer school. When she confronted
> me, I lied.
>
> I knew I had a problem with stealing and with
> honesty in general. Laura had witnessed my lying to
> this girl and tried to make me understand the trust
> involved.
>
> But several weeks later a different girl saw her
> bracelet on my bureau; I'd also taken that during
> summer school. Again I lied when confronted.
>
> This time, the look in Laura's eyes hurt the worst. I
> wanted to hold onto her and scream out how sorry I
> was. She spoke quietly and said again and again, "But
> we all trusted you; doesn't that mean anything to you?"
>
> The next three weeks were the loneliest I ever spent.
> Laura didn't speak to me. Every day it hurt more and
> more. For the first time I began to understand what it
> means to trust someone and be trusted and how
> precious that trust is.
>
> I think Laura knew how much she affected me by
> ignoring me. I felt numb to the words people said, but
> her silence cut like a knife.
>
> One night, lying in our beds, we finally started

talking. I told her about all of the feelings I'd kept
inside all year and how much I cared about her. I
could hardly talk, I was crying so hard; I just lay there
sniffling. I could hear her crying too. Those tears said
so much to me, and I think she knew that.

Then she said very seriously, "Helen?"

"Yeah," I said.

"Did you know that when you cry lying down, you
get puddles in your ears?"

Sure enough, I had them too. We both began to
laugh. That was all she needed to say.

Helen's bond with Laura helped her to "let go" of her
stealing and lying attitude. She ultimately graduated from
Hyde and pursued a successful teaching career.

Running from the Truth: Jack's Story

Unfortunately, not all students are able to face themselves
when confronted with the truth, as Kay discovered. Kay had
made great strides at Hyde after a turbulent past that included
a brief stay in a state mental hospital after a "knock-down-
drag-out fight" with her parents. Now she was trying to help
others with the lessons she'd struggled so hard to learn.

One day Kay confronted another student, Jack, about his
plagiarism of a short story for a term paper. She relates what
happened:

We were reading our term papers in English class so
others could evaluate them. When Jack read his, I had
a sinking feeling—I recognized it as a story I once
read. Because Mr. Hawley wasn't there, I told the
class. Jack said he hadn't copied it, that he had
worked very hard writing it and was offended I would
say such a thing.

I thought maybe years ago Jack read the story only
to forget it; maybe subconsciously he had remembered
parts, certain phrases, and such. But it festered in my
mind all day.

Finally that night I searched the library and found

the story. I stared at the book; it was word for word. My head spun.

Jack was in the next room. I had the story in my hand, with my finger holding the place. My face was hot and I was shaking and stuttering. I handed him the book and told him it was word for word. He again denied copying it, straight to my face. I threw up my hands and walked out.

I wasn't hurt that Jack lied to me. In a way I pitied him, not for what he did—I've done some pretty stupid things myself—but for what he didn't understand. In the shuffle to be something he wasn't he forgot what was really important.

Here is a classic confrontation between the values of Hyde and the values of the system. Jack is still caught up in the system's achievement ethic and in being "something that he wasn't." In spite of the many caring, close relationships he'd developed at Hyde, Jack couldn't trust that his new friends truly accepted him for what he was, and that they would view this incident, not as a chance to condemn or reject him, but as an opportunity for growth and a deepening of their relationship with him. Sadly, instead of facing his moment of truth, he literally ran away.

The Community Action Program

Eventually we extended the concept of Brother's Keeper to embrace the community outside the gates of Hyde, implementing our Community Action program. One serious limitation of America's educational system is that it consistently puts students in the receiving role. The Community Action program, which is a required part of the Hyde curriculum, places students in a giving role, enabling them to experience for themselves how their unique potential can make a difference in the lives of others.

Through the program, students have the opportunity to work with elementary school kids, the retarded, the elderly, the disabled, and others in the local community and beyond.

A teacher writes of students helping a local nursing home put on an anniversary party and dance:

> When we walked into the lounge, chairs and wheelchairs were in a small circle. The kids went from person to person, trying to push aside their own nervousness. Nobody knew quite what to do.
>
> I felt myself shy away from the invalids and move toward stronger people. I also avoided the woman who sat in the wheelchair, her legs folded beneath her like broken sticks, her head slumped to the side. It was clear she couldn't hold it up.
>
> As Tony approached her, she struggled to say something but couldn't get it out. She reached out her arms. "My name is Martha," she finally said. Tony seemed almost frozen.
>
> "Your name is what?" he asked, leaning a little closer. I could see the fear, the revulsion, but also the compassion in his eyes.
>
> She held out her hands, crying. Tony stepped forward and clasped her hands. So that she could take part in the dance, he simply swung her hands from side to side in time to the music. She couldn't talk and he didn't try to say anything.
>
> By this time our fear and inhibitions had fallen by the wayside. One woman, who had not been out of her walker for months, was invited to dance. The student helped her to her feet and held her so she wouldn't fall, moving slowly back and forth across the floor. Those who watched her from their chairs and wheelchairs were enraptured.
>
> As we left the party I could tell the kids were visibly moved, as I was. We talked about what grandparents meant to us, how isolated we were from the aged, and how some had given up while others were still fighting. We all wondered how we would handle our own old age.

Over the years the Brother's Keeper principle eventually spread to teachers, staff members, and parents. The concept makes the atmosphere at Hyde intense and some-times confrontational, but what strikes visitors most is the depth of love and concern generated by our relationships. We really do need to help others in order to help ourselves.

Rethinking Academic Requirements

While students were com-ing to grips with them-selves and their values, I was facing my own conflict between the principles we espoused at Hyde and the policies we implemented.

I began Hyde with the only educational program I knew—a traditional, solidly academic curriculum. But because I had committed Hyde to the concept of character rather than academic achievement, my conscience knew that time would inevitably bring a confrontation.

The confrontation came when his math teacher told me that Greg could not pass algebra. I had met Greg two years earlier, during Hyde's first year. The headmaster of another school had recommended Greg to Hyde, imagining we needed students badly enough not to look too closely at their track records.

Greg had failed the seventh, eighth, and ninth grades in a private school (although the school had moved him along anyway). After testing at Harvard he was found to have a subnormal IQ and was advised to avoid college-prep work.

Greg had quickly become confused during our interview. As his parents sat stiffly and their son stared blankly, I probed what he wanted out of life, how he saw himself, and asked other searching questions. His responses seemed to confirm what the Harvard test had indicated about his IQ.

But it was hard to determine the extent to which his horrendous experiences in the traditional school system might account for some of his apparent dullness. When I first met him, Greg was a totally defeated young man; his school had smothered his confidence by ignoring his needs and just moving him on.

I concluded the admissions interview by saying that if Greg would give his best to Hyde, and if his parents would overlook his academic work for a while, we could at least begin to help him rebuild his confidence. But, I added, because our own academic level might eventually be too high for Greg, we'd have to play it one year at a time.

Greg had flunked algebra before and proceeded to flunk it again. We required that he make up the work in our summer school but his skills were so weak that we ended up putting him in a fundamentals class. He repeated algebra in his sophomore year with a different teacher and was flunking badly again when I called him in to see for myself.

Greg and I pored over his algebra textbook and filled sheet after sheet of yellow paper with numbers. I had hoped that it was his teachers' approach that had failed, but as I probed Greg's understanding of the subject, I knew they were right: he couldn't pass Algebra I.

I smiled at Greg, put my hand on his shoulder, and said I'd see him later. After he'd left I knew my moment of truth had come; either I had to let Greg go in June or drop our algebra requirement for graduation.

I rose from my seat and walked to the fireplace to run my fingers over the words inscribed on the Hyde shield—Courage, Integrity, Concern, Curiosity, and Leadership—as if hoping they would transmit a message of guidance.

What choices did I have? I felt sure Greg could pass algebra if we completely retaught him math but how could I justify all that work just to meet one requirement? I could shake my head sadly and tell his parents that Greg just couldn't hack it, as I'd warned them, but wouldn't that compromise my commitment to find a better way for *all* kids?

In spite of his nickname "Goofy"—after the slow-witted comic strip character—Greg was the hardest worker in his class and showed enough spirit to be elected Freshman of the Year. That fall Greyhound Bus Lines had called his parents to report an episode in which a drunk had picked a fight with the driver and fifteen-year-old Greg had stepped forward from the back of the bus and ejected him. Here was a kid with plenty of courage and character. Isn't that what Hyde was supposed to be about?

But keeping Greg scared the hell out of me. Hyde had constantly fought the image of being a "problem kid school" because of our willingness to consider any student who was willing to make the commitment to our character–unique potential concept. To some people, accepting kids no one else would take meant that we couldn't be right for the "best" students.

Suppose I was misguided in my belief that effort and attitude alone could produce excellence, and Greg graduated someday to become just a pleasant "Goofy"? The educational grapevine would declare Hyde a school for "nice, dumb kids" and we'd never see any other kind of candidate again. At a deeper level than my fear of the grapevine, I was scared to let go of traditional academic standards. In spite of my criticisms, I respected academic excellence. Still, I was convinced there must be more to education than academic achievement.

Two years earlier, when the faculty had voted to reject a student on the basis of his work during our first summer school, I had decided to trust my instincts and risk taking him anyway. Larry eventually won our highest honor, the Hyde Award, and today is an independent school headmaster.

But it is one thing to take a risk on one kid and quite another to risk an entire school. I had to sink or swim with Greg. Finally, I made the decision to drop academic requirements for graduation at Hyde—actually, with a sigh of relief. Maybe we'd never stand for anything in the eyes of the world, I thought, but at least we would have the courage to be a truly democratic school by letting go of standards that depended primarily on one's inborn traits.

Our decision to put our faith in Greg helped him to rebuild his confidence in himself and his potential. When it came time for college, he was still sensitive about his academic ability but asked only that I help him choose a school where a top attitude and solid effort would help to ensure success.

Greg graduated from a New Hampshire college in three years with a 3.27 out of a possible 4.00 grade point average. Explaining his belated academic success, he commented, "When I found my academic background lacking in college, I compensated with my determination and was able to overcome difficult courses."

Greg never did pass algebra, but he quickly showed his leadership in business by shaping up a plant that employed eighty-five people and had serious morale problems. Eventually his trouble-shooting ability enabled him to become a top executive. It wasn't what he couldn't do but what he *could do* that counted.

Echoing the words of Marty at our victory celebration, Greg later wrote, "Just knowing someone believed in me set the background for many of my future achievements."

Concentrating on Attitude

The progress of kids like Greg encouraged me to ease up further on our traditional standards. I tried hard to get the school to move away from measuring growth by achievements that were the result of innate abilities. "Don't we all have abilities?" I hammered. "Are the abilities students have in school today the ones they'll need in the future?"

I had expected that Hyde's emphasis on character development would easily replace academic achievement as the standard by which students were evaluated. But because of America's confusion over the true role of character in the educational process, incoming students were totally unprepared for our new approach.

To shift students' focus from academic achievement, I began to concentrate on attitude: "Develop a constructive attitude," I told them. "Give your best effort to your work, and trust your potential to take care of the rest." I argued that the right attitude would maximize academic achievement.

To test my theory, I decided to try an experiment. I would

teach an Algebra III class and grade students on the development of a productive attitude toward learning, not on their academic achievement. If my theory was right, their attitude and effort would be reflected in higher math scores as well. To keep the experiment pure, I would use standardized tests, which would limit my control over the results.

Each student faced a different challenge. One very creative but disorganized student was graded on discipline and follow-through. A student who was overly teacher-dependent was graded on self-reliance. Another student who "couldn't do math" was graded on self-confidence; and so on. I flunked the top achiever until he demonstrated genuine curiosity and learned how to share his gift with others.

By Christmas the class's overall achievement scores were so terrible, I almost gave up my experiment. But fortunately my commitment to the concept forced me to continue. By June, test scores were dramatically improved, and the students' math accomplishments—in terms of their abilities—were some of the best in my teaching experience. By focusing on learning attitudes, I had found a way to unblock student fears of math, to fairly challenge each student personally, and then to motivate each one to learn math as a means to grow personally! Superior learning occurs when students not only realize they *can* learn but can further see how that learning really benefits *them*.

Challenging a "Model" Student

To develop the unique potential of students required that we present them with challenges. For students like Greg, this was an easy task. But for a handful of model students, such as Ken, finding a challenge was a challenge in itself.

Ken Grant was a local boy whose father worked at the Bath Iron Works. The only child of solid parents, Ken was the epitome of the "perfect" kid. Throughout his four years at Hyde, I don't remember a single episode that even hinted of any obvious character weakness—anger, selfishness, laziness, swelled head—you name it. He was the kind of person who always went after his best and tackled whatever you put in his path. He was number one in the class, the school's top distance runner, captain of the cross-country and track teams, an active participant in student government, and well liked by all.

But Ken's "perfect" Hyde career bothered me. True character must be forged by trial, so what had we done for Ken that couldn't have been done by any school? I couldn't shake the feeling that we were failing him.

I knew we would have to present Ken with a real challenge. No matter how well prepared we think we are, life is bound to throw us curves. If we don't test our mettle at an early age, we may not have the confidence to manage the trials we'll inevitably encounter later in life.

I did feel that Ken was too respectful of others, especially those in authority, and not enough of himself. If he were to become a truly responsible, self-governing adult, he would have to learn to respect his own inner authority.

As a test, I instructed Ken to go out and violate Hyde's code of ethics. Several years later, I asked a group of Hyde graduates, Ken among them, to write about their meaningful experiences. Here is some of what he wrote about the challenge I posed:

> Perhaps the most meaningful experience in my life came one October morning when I walked into Mr. Gauld's office to ask for a recommendation for college. . . . I distinctly remember his looking deeply into my eyes and saying, "Ken, you need a challenge and struggle. I want you to go out and do something against your creeds and values, then come back and let me know how you feel." This statement was forceful and direct; Mr. Gauld left no option.
>
> I left his office totally perplexed and scared. I remember as I walked down the hall how my eyes got misty. I can't remember the next few days.
>
> I do recall telling my parents, I guess looking for comfort and support. I didn't get it. They both were perplexed, but my mother's only reply was, "Well, what are you going to do?"
>
> I struggled within, only telling one or two of my closest friends about the talk. A week passed and I still hadn't done anything; my conscience wouldn't let me. Yet I kept thinking how Mr. Gauld wanted and demanded that I follow through. But each day passed and I failed to follow through.
>
> Finally, I just had to talk with Mr. Gauld. I was really scared, probably visibly so. After all, I was defying his authority.
>
> I simply said, "Mr. Gauld, I can't do what you ask; my conscience won't let me." I was ready for lightning to strike. Yet the only response from Mr. Gauld was a huge smile, full of warmth and love. To say the least, I was totally perplexed. I just couldn't grasp the meaning of our encounter.

Years later the meaning became clearer to Ken:

> I found college a struggle. No longer were my grades among the highest or my athletic ability among the

finest. I had few distinctions to separate me from the others. I was just quiet, well-liked, good-natured Ken.

In my first two years, struggling in college's academic and athletic intensity, I spent little time reflecting on what I was doing. Then by my junior and senior years, I began to realize something . . . I was being intimidated by college.

I was doing what was expected of me, not to please just myself, but my professors and coaches. I would give 100 percent of myself to them, but I'd only get 20 percent in return.

I began to question their attitudes, accountability, and authority. I became actively involved in student groups struggling to make someone accountable for our education. In short, college and authority no longer intimidated me.

This experience finally explained my encounter with Mr. Gauld. He knew that Hyde's ethical codes were basic to my life. Yet he also knew that authority intimidated me. So he challenged me to stand on my own two feet and demand respect for my being. I now understand Mr. Gauld's smile and realize the strength within me.

In fact, I hadn't been sure of what I was trying to prove by my experiment; I was merely following my deeper instincts. I did what I thought was right, he did what he thought was right, and our consciences created a beautiful teaching experience! I am almost ashamed to take any credit; Ken and I were simply spectators to a drama being played out by "powers greater than ourselves."

Equal Opportunity (and Treatment) for All

Most of the students who attended Hyde were from families that could afford the luxury of sending their teenagers to private school. But we tried, within our financial limits, to open the doors of Hyde to *any* kid who could make the commitment to seek his or her best.

With that commitment in mind, we took money out of our annual budget to develop scholarship programs for inner-city kids in six cities. These young people had been sadly neglected by the system. Consider Bill, Clarence, and Phil, three kids who came to us from Cleveland's inner city.

Bill, a former gang leader (at age eleven) who came from what one observer called "the toughest street in America," began in our ninth grade unable to spell even three-letter words. On a test to identify the fifty states, Clarence could only locate Ohio, where he was from, and Maine, where Hyde is located. (My son, Malcolm, remarked: "At least he knows where he's been and where he's going.") In an essay describing himself and his dreams, Phil wrote a total of four lines. When I called him on the carpet for his meager effort, suggesting in no uncertain terms that he wasn't even trying, he looked at me and said, sincerely, "Thanks. Nobody ever told me that."

I'm not surprised. Unfortunately, I've watched teachers intensely confront the "spoiled brat" attitudes of a privileged suburban kid, and then become strangely tolerant of the belligerent defensiveness of some kid from the ghetto. In their misguided attempts at demonstrating concern, these teachers send a clear message: we expect a great deal from the suburbanite, but the ghetto kid really should feel sorry for himself.

I constantly have to remind teachers, parents, and students of this deeper truth: We've all been given the right hand to play in life; if we have the courage to play the deuces and threes, we'll eventually find the kings and aces.

Bill, Clarence, and Phil were all successes at Hyde, and all three went on to college. I must add that two of these kids had dedicated mothers behind them; and the third, a committed grandfather. Given family support—a concept so crucial I'll devote three chapters (5 through 7) to it—all they needed was a school-community that honestly expected as much from their children as from any other kid.

Confronting Albert

At Hyde, all students receive equal treatment, whether they come from wealthy neighborhoods or the heart of the ghetto.

When I first met Albert, I didn't know anything about his inner-city background, or the feeling he had described in a school paper—of being "some log that's kicked around." I just saw a kid who was used to protecting himself and who, like any kid, will get things on his own terms if you let him.

One day in basketball, Albert refused to take off his shirt when his team was designated "skins." When I said that we wouldn't reverse uniforms for his sake, he (incredibly) replied that everyone could simply tell which team he was on.

I finally put my nose an inch from his and said, "Albert, you either take that shirt off or go pack your bags and take the next bus home." I knew he was probably self-conscious about something underneath his shirt (it turned out to be a roll of fat); but kids should not feel shame about themselves, and I knew that Albert had been at Hyde long enough to test his trust in us.

Our eyes seemed interminably riveted in a silent confrontation. Finally, Albert slowly began to take off his shirt.

The system had unwittingly helped Albert to be overly sensitive about his feelings, thus making him unable to determine where his true self ended and his unproductive attitudes began. Albert was ashamed of his body, and he had learned to manipulate his teachers in order to hide that shame; this had been easy, because no one was willing to confront the "poor kid from the ghetto." As a result, Albert secretly believed he wasn't as good as other kids and had never learned to accept himself.

Although Albert's ego was bruised in our confrontation, his deeper wisdom responded to my concern. Regardless of the obvious gaps of understanding caused by our different skin colors, backgrounds, and ages, he knew I could be trusted, and now he began to accept himself and trust in his own unique potential.

This confrontation marked the beginning of a deep spiritual relationship between us. At the end of his junior year, after graduation ceremonies, Albert—who had been so defiant on the basketball court—approached me, tears streaming down his face, and without a word put his arms around me.

CHAPTER 3

Growing Pains

Everyone thinks of changing the world,
but no one thinks of changing himself.
— Leo Tolstoy

By the spring of our third year, the faculty had become more sensitive to the many attitudes holding back the senior class. So we sent the entire class on a week-long outdoor retreat to examine themselves more closely and relate to one another at a deeper level. At the conclusion of this experiment the students gave one another written descriptions of their feelings. The papers were honestly done and proved a humbling experience for many.

Don and Ray, two of the boys on the retreat, had failed in high school and had come to Hyde as very unhappy individuals. While at Hyde, they became high achievers: both had done well academically, had been accepted to good colleges, were viewed as school leaders, and, as wrestling captains, had led their team to second place in the New England championships. But according to the papers written by their peers, they were particularly selfish individuals.

Don and Ray refused to accept the evaluations of their classmates. Now that they possessed the academic success that had previously eluded them in the system, why did they need to change just to please their classmates and Hyde School?

After they returned from their retreat, I told Don and Ray that we planned to work on attitude in the spring term; if they were satisfied with theirs, I saw no reason for them to stay at Hyde. We could certify their credits for college, but unless they were willing to change their attitudes and commit themselves to real growth, not just academic and athletic achievement, they would not receive a Hyde diploma or participate in graduation ceremonies.

I suggested both boys go home and talk to their parents before making a final decision. I felt confident of parental support; Don's mother had once said to me, "I don't know what you've got, but I wish you could bottle it."

Initially the two families seemed determined to talk some sense into their sons, although they had some difficulty in understanding the problem. But one afternoon I found both sets of parents waiting to see me in my office. I knew from the grim expressions on their faces that I was in for a battle.

Don's father, an articulate executive, told me firmly, "Joe, we're not here for any lectures on philosophy. Don and Ray are fine products of this school and certainly deserve diplomas. We're not leaving until we have them."

I held my ground, and the crisis eventually went to the Board of Trustees. In the end, the two families left and the Hyde diploma remained uncompromised. But the confrontation signaled the growing conflict of values between Hyde and the educational system outside its gates.

Despite the boys' unhappiness at their previous schools, their successes at Hyde, and even Don's admission after the retreat that "I guess when all twenty-four classmates say you have a problem with selfishness, arrogance, and defensiveness, it must be true," the boys' parents still chose to trust academic achievement over our total commitment to their sons' unique potential. The influence of the system was a powerful adversary to the growth of the Hyde concept.

The Student "Bust"

After being preoccupied with battling adults and the educational system, I suddenly had to recognize another powerful adversary—a new level of alienation in the students themselves. Although Don and Ray chose to follow their parents and bet on the system's values, the 1960s saw growing disenchantment among America's youth. Their lack of confidence in adult leadership finally led them to spawn an underground culture that emphasized drugs, sex ("free love"), and "doing your own thing."

The conflict between Hyde and the youth culture finally erupted on campus in our fourth year with the student "bust" of 1970. At Hyde we define a bust as a basic confrontation between our actions and our stated beliefs, usually involving a group of people. It becomes a schoolwide accounting of transgressions, which enables the clearing of consciences, the honoring of accountability, and a new start with a clean slate. (One student describes it as "Drano for the Hyde soul.")

The bust occurred with the breakdown of our honor code in the spring. Students had no trouble agreeing to "no lying, cheating, or stealing," but our rules about "no smoking, drinking, or drugs" confronted their culture, and many students, under pressure from friends outside Hyde, violated that part of the honor code.

I had sensed that something was wrong after spring break, and I confronted the students. When the dust settled, it turned out that, of the 117 students at Hyde, 102 were at least indirectly involved. About a third had actually violated one of our smoking-drinking-drugs rules, with the rest knowing of violations but failing to report them as they were required to do.

Part of the reason these widespread violations went unreported had to do with the penalties we imposed at the time. The first time a student was caught smoking or drinking, he was put on probation; the next time, the student was expelled. Drug use meant automatic expulsion. It was one thing for a student to turn in a friend who would only be disciplined; it was quite another to feel responsible for having the friend forced out of Hyde.

The reasons for the violations themselves ran deeper. To understand what had gone wrong, the faculty spent more than thirty hours interviewing every student at Hyde. A larger truth began to emerge, perceptively explained by one student: "Looking back, I had a lot of respect for the administration and teachers at Hyde, but in my zeal to please them, I was afraid of bringing up the subject of sex or drugs. The faculty always encouraged us to be honest and open. But when drugs and sex became a big part of my generation, the faculty balked, and we students skirted the issue. I would have felt guilty disclosing my feelings on those subjects to my teachers; I thought that would somehow tarnish our relationship."

The interviews reaffirmed the desire of students to believe in Hyde and in themselves. But they also made it clear that students simply couldn't balance the behavior expected under our honor code with the behavior expected by their friends outside the gates of Hyde.

We, the faculty, were doing nothing to help students resist this outside peer pressure; in fact, we had been avoiding the issue altogether, hiding behind the honor code. Students would break the code and, just when they needed us most, would have to distance themselves from us and become part of an ever-growing band of "outlaws," until the conflict came to a head. Although it was the students who had compromised themselves and the school, it was obvious that both sides needed to make some changes.

We had been guilty of allowing students to accept more responsibility than we'd prepared them to handle. But the deeper problem was allowing a system—even an honor system—to dictate the growth of individuals. Instead of the honor code assisting in students' growth, it was in many cases hindering that growth.

I resolved never again to let some program—any program—dictate our actions. Unique potential was our goal at Hyde, and its development should be the complete responsibility of the individuals involved. So we resolved to rely solely on the individual commitment made by each teacher, student, and parent during the interview, rather than on an external honor code.

A Money-Back Guarantee

Hyde dropped the honor code and developed a money-back guarantee: If a student walked out on his or her commitment, we would keep the full tuition. But if the school wanted to expel a student, we would have to return the entire tuition. If the student and his parents followed our program and were not satisfied with the results by the end of the school year in June, we would be obligated to return the full tuition.

This guarantee put the burden of student progress on faculty as well as parents and students. If students chose to walk out of Hyde, it was their responsibility. But if they chose to stay, it was our responsibility to help them grow, no matter what their infractions or however seemingly "impossible" their attitudes. When a teacher complained of an "unteachable" student, I would ask rhetorically, "Shall we return the tuition?"

This guarantee made our acceptance interview even more intense, because both sides were agreeing to back up their commitment with financial liability. The guarantee stripped away rationalizations and social niceties to lay bare the gut issues of growth. We pulled no punches in the interview. If a parent or a student objected to our approach, we simply said, "Do it anyway; if it doesn't work, you can get your money back in June." Sometimes a candidate would storm out of the interview in the first five minutes. Later, it might be a parent. Sometimes the one who left would come back the next day and apologize. One candidate was accepted on the fifth interview after flunking the first four.

It never failed to amaze me that the process of helping a kid find his or her own best was often a constant battle. Why did parents and students resist our efforts to help them become honest and to learn to trust who they truly were? It is a sad commentary that even with our rigorous interview, our six-week summer trial, and our guarantee that we would return the entire tuition if either we expelled the student or the family was ultimately unsatisfied, we still had students who reneged on their commitment and ran away.

If parents remained firm and gave their offspring the choice of returning to Hyde or going away on their own, instead of letting them come home, we were ultimately successful. But despite our careful interview process and our guarantees, roughly 15 percent of all Hyde parents folded on their commitment, and their children never finished the school year. Although we never had to refund a tuition and expelled just one student (who later returned to graduate), the guarantee was discontinued in 1986. We found that in the toughest cases parents still resisted change and expected Hyde's guarantee magically to make it all work.

But whatever our concerns about parents, the honesty and concern we displayed in the aftermath of the student bust had led students to trust Hyde on a much deeper level. Little did I realize then that we would first have to experience a *faculty* bust before we could fully honor that trust.

Strengthening the Commitment to Unique Potential

During the student bust, we had been in the process of undergoing evaluation for accreditation by the New England

Association of Colleges and Secondary Schools. The Visiting Committee, which later approved our accreditation, helped us realize the bust was in reality a confirmation that the Hyde concept worked. Bolstered by their encouragement, including a statement that "older institutions could learn something from this relatively new school, that if character could be developed, then academic achievement up to the level of one's potential will follow . . . ," I committed myself to strengthening Hyde's character–unique potential curriculum.

First, I was determined that no subject or lesson would be more sacred than a student's unique potential; even something as seemingly sound as the honor code had ended up compromising student growth. Learning must first be built on a bond between teacher and student; the purpose of the subject was to help develop one's unique potential. To help break traditional subject orientation, I experimented in summer school by having the math teachers teach English and the English teachers math. Learning actually increased! The experience also helped teachers to realize they had more to give as student-teachers than as "professors."

Second, I believed the student's life itself should be the first "subject" of the teacher. The bust had revealed that sex and drugs, the chief preoccupations of the students' generation, went unmentioned because the faculty were self-conscious and avoided these issues. If Hyde were to be a true preparation for life, we could never again allow such a gap between the world of the teachers and the world of the students.

Third, teachers would need to share their own lives in order to forge a stronger student-teacher bond. Because the system rewarded subject knowledge and not the understanding of and commitment to growing children, it encouraged teachers to carve out their own piece of turf and just concern themselves with that. Teachers would have to give more of themselves in order to bring out the unique potential and character of their students. Little did I know the resistance I would face in attempting to require the faculty to share more of themselves with their students and with one another.

The Faculty "Bust"

We had found that seminars, in which students shared their hopes, fears, strengths, weaknesses, problems, and experiences with one another, were a powerful vehicle for growth. I had instituted a senior seminar in 1970. In 1971 I invited some faculty members to attend, and in time the seniors sensitively and objectively began to discuss the faculty's teaching strengths and weaknesses with them. Teachers were reminded whenever they strayed too often from the subject or were too controlling or not challenging enough. Every teacher claimed to find the evaluations meaningful, thought-provoking, and surprisingly perceptive.

Therefore, I introduced a faculty seminar in which teachers could share their professional and personal lives with one another. The seminar seemed a natural and necessary step, because we had already established the need for teachers to lead by example. But once the seminar was underway, the mood changed. As the group began to delve deeper into their lives, some teachers resisted, and a faculty split began to emerge.

Program Director Bud Warren writes of this period:

> The faculty obviously were in the midst of the struggle. The issue was commitment. Joe seemed always to be there, relentlessly trying to get us to look beyond and ahead, to deal with the truth of our lives, and share that truth with one another and the kids—just what we were asking of them.
>
> The bulk of the group seemed personally threatened; one called Joe a "dangerous man," another a "religious fanatic"; others said he was unfair, unfeeling, egomaniacal, or simply sick. It was tough, one argued, to change a lifetime of work with kids and have to start in again at ground zero, not only in the hierarchy of a new school but also in a sense of commitment.
>
> And the faculty didn't trust one another. One argued, "I'd ask kids to open up their lives and share deeply with one another, but it's unhealthy and dangerous for grown adults to risk that sort of openness with one another. The kids are growing; we're already formed as individuals." (!)

Finally, one faculty group went to the trustees to insist that I be given a leave of absence in 1971. When the full case was aired, the trustees supported my position, and even though a third of the faculty left that June, those who remained were ready to "burn the boats" and trust the demands the new curriculum would make on them.

It is disturbing to note that the teachers most experienced in the system had been the most threatened by our new process. Their confidence in subject mastery seemed divorced from their confidence in themselves and their deeper beliefs. Disturbing, because, in the words of Kahlil Gibran, the true teacher "gives not of this wisdom but of his faith and his lovingness."

Our faculty bust broke down the barrier to a deeper student-teacher bond. After the bust, teachers were perceived more as growing, fallible individuals than as the font of all knowledge. This recognition opened the door for students to accept more responsibility for the teaching and learning process.

Teacher Evaluations

Before Christmas in 1972, when Hyde was six years old, we decided to have the entire school evaluate the attitude and effort of each student in all courses, sports, financial management, dorm life, and work duties. The entire process took six hours and resulted in a report card for Hyde.

The experience was so impressive that we decided to ask the entire student body to do teacher evaluations. Teachers would sit on the stage while students evaluated their strengths and weaknesses, the essence of what each was teaching, and the areas in which each needed to improve. Once teachers weathered the cultural shock of the experience, they found a new ally with a surprisingly deep understanding of their true potential.

The "Hot Seat"

In the summer of 1973, after Paul Hurd had graduated from Bowdoin and completed graduate work at the University of Chicago, he returned to Hyde for a teaching internship. His teaching experience and subsequent evaluation by students left a powerful impression on him:

> In my first week as a Hyde intern I quickly discovered that my relationships with kids needed a more responsible and serious approach than my summer as a Hyde counselor had prepared me for. Simply taking an attitude of warmth and concern didn't necessarily mean that students like Barry, a loud, self-indulgent, strong-willed seventeen-year-old from an exclusive Boston suburb, would fall all over themselves to listen to me.
>
> My first head-on collision with students occurred in the second week, when three members of my

counseling group decided they didn't like my selection of a group activity and decided to sit it out. I was panic-stricken. Now what? Coax? Command? I began by asking a neutral question:

"What's the problem?"

"Nothing, we're just too tired."

"Well, don't you think others in the group are tired?"

"They can sit down if they want to."

"Yeah, but they aren't. The others are trying to stick together and help one another out."

My handle on neutrality was evaporating. Michelle hit me with an icy stare and a surly tone: "Well, that's their problem."

Boom! My lid went off and I yelled: "Get up and get over there!" Perhaps out of sheer surprise, the three jumped up and moved as one back to the group.

As the weeks wore on I put less confidence in myself and more in this drill sergeant method of getting things done. But my table at evening meals became the last to fill and the first to empty, and I noticed many kids change their direction when they saw me approaching.

I tried to console myself with the handful of kids who did stick around: Cindi, with her sensitivity and unhesitating trust; Matt, humorous and genuinely concerned for his peers; and Millie, an orphan from New York City, full of pride and gutsy determination. I wanted to tell all of them how much they gave me, but somehow my own insecurities wouldn't let me.

I learned a tremendous respect for kids and their potential for growth through sharing their experiences and struggles—like the night we portaged six loaded canoes for five miles, then paddled another eight against the current. But the most forceful and pressing lesson of the summer came in the final week, when the students evaluated the faculty. The prospect raised a vague gnawing in my stomach.

Joe began with the most seasoned teachers. As the evaluations progressed, I was continually struck by the perception and concern expressed by even the toughest "problem kids" of the summer. As each faculty member described his or her own feelings and then received student reactions, I became freshly aware of a sensitivity and integrity in the kids I'd never taken advantage of because of my own lack of openness and trust.

Finally Joe called me to the "hot seat" and I sat down and looked into a sea of faces whose eyes went straight through me. Joe asked for comments on my strengths, and perhaps half a dozen hands went up:

"Dependable . . . forceful . . . demands respect."

Then he asked for weaknesses. A mass of hands were waving in front of me. The comments that followed shook my self-esteem to the core:

"Cold . . . too harsh . . . hard to get to know . . . cares only about what he is doing . . . hard to talk to . . . bad temper . . . does not try to understand people . . . needs a lot of help."

It took a great effort for me to go back to my seat. I was shocked. The remainder of the evaluation didn't register with me at all. I just sat there, dazed amid a blur of voices.

Everything around me had a strange coldness as I walked back to my apartment. I lay down on my bed and blankly stared at the ceiling. Was teaching really my destiny? Was I attempting something I was simply not cut out for?

I had asked to talk to Joe, and he sent word for me to see him after dinner that evening. I both dreaded and craved his reaction and advice. I knew from the past that he wouldn't protect me from anything I needed to face.

I walked into his office and sat down. He wheeled around from behind his desk and sat down in a chair right across from me. I braced myself.

"You got a pretty tough evaluation today, Paul," he said. "How do you feel?"

"Pretty shook. Right now I'm not sure how to sort the whole thing out. I knew there's plenty personally that I need to change, but I'm also wondering if I should be reconsidering going into teaching."

Joe smiled and leaned forward: "You may be overreacting. A lot of the message to you out there today was for you to loosen up more. In attempting to establish your authority, you've submerged the warmer, and at times more vulnerable, side that those who know you well trust and respect. To be a truly effective teacher you must expect to struggle and share your growth in the same way the kids do. Today has given you a good indication of your next step in growing as a teacher."

The Spiritual Teacher

Paul's evaluation shows what a powerful untapped resource students can be for teacher development. The summer school students themselves had only been at Hyde for eight weeks, yet they were able to correctly point Paul in the right direction for his professional growth in just a ten-minute session, one he would never forget. Education is the students' occupation, and they can be just as capable of professional pride as are doctors and lawyers.

The evaluation was a painful experience for Paul. But just as his humility allowed him to take the students' criticism deeply to heart, so did his courage allow him to heed its lessons and leave my office with a new determination.

Helping youngsters develop their unique potential and character is by far the most demanding job of all. I can't imagine a more rewarding experience, but teachers should make no mistake about the psychological cost. They must be fully prepared to deal with the truth about their own character, commitment, abilities, even their marriage and family relationships—in short, about any and every aspect of their lives.

Such self-examination is crucial to becoming what I call a "spiritual" parent or teacher, one who helps youngsters to develop and believe in their unique potential. Parents and teachers must look deeply within themselves before they are capable of helping their children or students do the same.

In 1985, Paul Hurd had a successful career as historical coordinator for the state of Ohio. I asked him to return as Hyde's director of studies. During the next three years, I noticed that students still hesitated over his demanding standards, but they trusted his concern and even treated his toughness with humor.

As I finished this chapter we had just completed graduation—a deeply spiritual time at Hyde, when every graduating senior speaks. I noted that four of our graduates thanked Paul specifically for his faith in them.

Paul's evaluation in 1973 was like a report card for Hyde School. Students were obviously absorbing the concepts of attitude, character, and even unique potential, confirmed by their capacity to help one of their teachers. Beyond the founder and the faculty, the school itself was now teaching the students.

CHAPTER 4

The Path
to Excellence

I hear—and I forget;
I see—and I remember;
But I do—and I understand.
—Chinese proverb

W e have found there is a natural progression of growth that all Hyde students seem to follow. It involves three distinct stages: motions, effort, and excellence. My son, Malcolm, describes how he first observed these stages of growth during the course of coaching a girls' soccer team at Hyde:

I coached the girls' soccer team in the fall of 1985. It was a sport I'd never played, and it didn't grab my soul like basketball or lacrosse. But I've always taken athletics seriously and had high hopes that fall—hopes that were severely challenged at the very first practice.

The twenty-odd girls in front of me had no interest in soccer. Not only did they not want to play soccer, they held great disdain for Hyde's mandatory sports policy, which was the only reason they showed up in the first place.

None was a genuine athlete, and all of them looked better suited for a rock concert than a soccer practice. Jewelry glistened in abundance. There were punk haircuts, and torn and tattered T-shirts, some very suggestive. Most girls wore makeup and several had carefully and extensively styled their hair. Some had even brought their purses to the playing field.

Clearly these girls were not soccer players and had no interest in becoming such. I felt like the kid who must clean up his room, but it's so messy he doesn't know where to begin.

So, my early message was simple: "From the start we're going to go through the motions that serious soccer players go through. Serious players show up on time for practice. They dress with some semblance of uniformity (I purchased reversible T-shirts). They have serious expressions when they do drills (we instilled the 'no "tee-hee"' rule: players were forbidden to laugh at a mistake because this is merely a defense mechanism). They encourage one another. They do wind sprints at the end of practice. They then put the balls away . . ." and so forth.

I didn't feel like a coach. All I could do at this point

was to lay out these simple expectations and make the alternative to fulfilling them even more distasteful: If someone was late to practice, the entire group would have to run extra sprints. Every practice would be extended until satisfactory effort materialized. A good work week meant a free weekend; otherwise the team would practice on Saturday.

I wasn't teaching much soccer. Not surprisingly, we failed to win a single contest or even to score a goal until the fifth game of the season.

Morale was low. My players despised me and routinely called home complaining to their parents about me. I received scowls when I met them in the hall, and I was the butt of jokes emanating from different corners of the campus. I found myself fondly remembering my previous teams that won games routinely. I began to doubt myself.

Then, slowly but surely, progress came. Team members actually began to compete for starting positions as if saying "as long as there's no way out of this sport, playing is more fun than watching." The few girls who did score a goal admitted they enjoyed the sensation and wanted more.

I was pleasantly surprised that the girls wanted to perform well in front of their parents on Parent's Weekend. Some of them sincerely seemed to want to improve. Nevertheless, I didn't have a lot to say at the fall sports banquet.

I coached boys' basketball in the winter and looked forward to brighter prospects. During the winter a group of local women formed an indoor soccer league using our field house as home base. I was startled when five Hyde girls asked if I could get them on a team in this league—the same girls who had earlier professed no interest in soccer! Yet, here they were, pursuing the sport on their own initiative. They got banged around considerably, but I was proud of them and my hopes for next September increased.

The second season came together like a fairy tale. Most girls returned for preseason practice of their own

volition. Veterans enforced standards among the new players, and I began to introduce more sophisticated soccer techniques and strategies. It became "cool" to try hard and "uncool" to exhibit those previous negative attitudes.

I feared playing the Bowdoin College jayvees at our opening game, but the team wanted to give it a go. We were clobbered, but high spirits prevailed anyway. Then we won our first league game against an old rival, and you'd have thought we'd won the Super Bowl! The girls discovered they loved to win and wanted to make it a habit.

That year, we emerged champions in the Maine Independent School League! The team's confidence snowballed to the point where I actually had to tone it down a bit. Winning was exciting, but more important, the girls had evolved into a group in pursuit of excellence—a lesson they could draw on when their soccer days were over.

This experience led me to believe that Hyde students go through three basic steps on the path of growth: motions, effort, and excellence. The teacher guides the process but must be willing to let go as students mature. I first controlled almost every aspect of the soccer team, but as the athletes moved toward the effort and excellence stages, I became more of an adviser.

As students complete the cycle of growth, they take on an obligation to teach the new initiates the motions of responsible behavior. Many students have told me they gain as much from this teaching step as they did when they were unenthusiastic learners.

The Three Stages of Growth

The three stages of growth—motions, effort, and excellence—are the gateways through which all students must pass in order to reach the ultimate goal of a Hyde School diploma, which signifies, *This individual is ready to conduct his or her life according to standards of personal excellence.* As students move through the stages, they exhibit a progressively higher level of effort, interest, and involvement:

- Motions: demonstrating that you can do what is expected of you
- Effort: demonstrating both your desire and competency to do it well
- Excellence: establishing your independence by uniformly seeking your best

Each stage can be thought of as a building block, a foundation on which the next stage is built. As students move through the stages, they gradually make the transition from being takers to becoming givers.

The Motions Stage: "Just Do It"

The emphasis in the motions stage is simply on doing whatever is required, not necessarily understanding it, liking it, or even agreeing with it. At this level, we only expect youngsters to imitate or act like responsible students. When they do, the results teach them why and motivate them to go on to the effort stage.

If they resist, Hyde is responsible for ensuring they go through the motions. This may require a few "five-thirties":

getting up early to do physical exercise and work. It may even take a "two-four": withdrawing from all activities, day and night, to join a work crew, thus providing a period of time for deeper personal reflection. In more severe cases, it may require an "attitude trip": a three- to seven-day retreat to an island, where students work together with others who have similar attitude problems.

Finally, it may even necessitate a youngster's decision to leave Hyde and go out on his or her own, allowing life to become the teacher. However, this is seldom necessary when parents retain their commitment to Hyde, and the family and Hyde work together; with this kind of cooperation the process has yet to fail.

Desystemization

The three stages of growth guide the development of unique potential. But the process is made more difficult by students' previous training in the system, which is essentially alien to the concepts of character and unique potential.

For this reason, the first step in the motions stage is "desystemization," a process by which we help students rid themselves of the unproductive habits and attitudes learned in the system. It is only after desystemization that kids can begin to reach for the unique potential that lies within.

Desystemization takes place during the six-week Summer Challenge program that most students attend before beginning their formal training at Hyde in the fall. Part of the process involves overcoming the results of the permissiveness that our self-indulgent society strongly encourages in American parenting.

Today I seldom see cases where parental strictness is robbing kids of spirit, but I am deluged by youngsters with so little expected of them that they have no idea of their potential or the meaning of their lives. Lacking any such guidance, they are easily brainwashed into seeking self-gratification, sensation, and other superficial goals with which the advertising world seduces them. Young people's natural urges for sex and exploration have been so exploited that their minds and feelings are no longer their own.

Here is a sample of the summer school talk I used to deliver to wake up new students:

> You don't think you're brainwashed? The cigarette companies have convinced you that smoking is a measure of your maturity. I'm trying to fight these neighborhood pushers and you end up getting mad at me for taking away your God-given right to smoke!
>
> The clothes and cosmetic industries make a bundle on you by seducing you into believing your goal in life is to be sexually desirable. You spend your whole week sniffing around to make out on Saturday night, all for the glory of that five-second orgasm, or just for the joy of getting wasted.
>
> No, you're not brainwashed. I stand here talking about your lives and your futures, and your eyelids droop. But let me say "drugs" and *boing!*, or "sex" and *boing!*—you're sitting up straight and every fiber in your bodies comes alive.
>
> And how did you become so insecure? You boys resemble a herd of seals who fight over turf and mates, and you girls accept that you are somebody else's property.
>
> Can't you exist without being in a clique? Would you sell your self-respect rather than be ostracized?

Kids resent being called brainwashed, but they recognize there is truth in my words.

"Hyde Is Like Listerine"

The desystemization process is highly effective, even in the case of kids who have been notorious troublemakers in the past, like Jim. After Jim was expelled from his high school for repeatedly cutting classes and breaking the school's no-smoking rule, his mother read an editorial about Hyde School. After an interview Jim was given a trial in our summer program and underwent desystemization.

A year later we wrote his parents: "We believe Jim will not only continue to grow at Hyde but will also be an asset to the community. . . . Jim is well on his way to becoming a young man of conscience and character."

How could a problem student like Jim make such a transformation in just a year? Jim's mother helps to explain, in a letter she wrote to her local newspaper about her son's summer school experience at Hyde.*

> Last spring you wrote an editorial about Hyde School. . . . About this time my son was expelled from G. High School. . . . His father took him for the required interview, and both made a commitment to Hyde.
>
> During the eight weeks that followed, weekly calls were made home: "Get me out of here, these kids rat on each other"; "Our canoe was swamped by a wave, and my tennis shoes are at the bottom of the ocean"; "We nearly starved on the ocean course in the dory" (ate all their provisions too soon and had only apples left the last day); then there were the pits dug "to bury the old image in" (my son's math class figured he dug enough dirt to cover an acre), not to mention work crews, being a shadow (having to constantly follow around some more responsible student), and what the kids termed the worst punishment, banishing a student to live by himself until he could prove he was ready to join the group again.
>
> All of these experiences brought this group of 120 kids to the realization Hyde had a lot to offer them. They found they could get along without cigarettes, lose weight or a bad image, overcome shyness, etc. A more confident, thoughtful, happy group emerged, visibly proud of their accomplishments.
>
> My son had no intention of returning to Hyde in the fall and was one of the last to decide to go back. . . . He confided he was not sure he hadn't been brainwashed. Finally, he said he thought Hyde was like Listerine: you hate it, but you know you need it.

---

* This was written in the early 1970s when we were experimenting with a variety of techniques to get through to kids. Many of our methods have since been greatly refined.

The system lulls students into believing that learning is a process of the mind alone; the caricature of today's schools is a classroom where silent rows of students listen to a talking adult. But we have found that growth involves not just the intellect but the heart, body, and soul as well. Providing students with new experiences generates new thinking, which in turn leads to new actions and behaviors. This cycle of action and reflection is far more effective than simple book learning in producing change.

When they first come to Hyde, kids think it is ridiculous to be put on work crew to do more productive thinking—until they do it. As the proverb says, I do—and I understand.

The process of desystemization may sound harsh, and it's true that during this stage we are often confrontational with kids' attitudes, but our commitment to our students' growth forms a strong bond of trust between us. Most of them come to understand that we are only trying to help them shed the barnacles from their true potential. (They also know we expect the same commitment from teachers and parents that we require of them.)

The Effort Stage: Brother's Keeper

A rule of thumb for recognizing true learning is this: Growth begets growth. As a Hyde student once observed, when one person moves or grows, the vibrations spread out like ripples in a pond to engulf others. So when a student really learns something, we should expect to see him give it to someone else; this is the foundation of the Brother's Keeper principle.

Beyond Desystemization: Jim and Mike

After Jim's rough summer of being desystemized, he slowly moved into the effort stage. In the story Jim tells below, we can see his transformation from the stubborn teen who derided our Brother's Keeper principle to a mature young man who is now exhibiting the desire and competency to help other students find the best in themselves:

> I had had a pretty confusing year, being forced into a lot of situations with my friends that I didn't like. Like with Mike: Mike was smoking and I knew it. We were very good friends; I had stayed at his house, knew his parents, and so on.
>
> I didn't want to risk our friendship, but I also knew he'd get out of Hyde feeling like he got nothing if I didn't. Plus I liked Mike a lot and wanted what was best for him even if he didn't.
>
> In the end I made him turn himself in. Within a few weeks he decided to leave the school.
>
> I walked over to his room and found him packing. I told him if he left he would be telling me, our friend David, a lot of other people, and himself to go to hell. I also called him a chicken and a lot of other things. We got into a battle of words, and then he said he didn't give a damn about me and David.
>
> I jumped on him, and we wrestled for about five minutes. I was crying a lot and so was he, and when we quit he just got up and left. Now, no matter what Michael does, at least I know I did my best for him.

When Jim came to Hyde he was still indoctrinated in the belief that "concern" means "I don't rat on my buddies," so he initially ignored Mike's smoking. But as he moved into the effort stage and began to pursue his own best he became committed to the best in his friends as well.

Passing on a Lesson: Albert and Kelly

After my confrontation with Albert on the basketball court, he started taking himself more seriously and, like Jim, began to take responsibility for passing along to others the lessons he'd learned in the motions stage.

Kelly, another black student, tells how Albert confronted his macho, tough-guy attitude, in much the same way that I had confronted Albert:

> Uncle Tom—that's what I said to myself when I first met Albert. Hyde had changed him; his black hide was

engraved in a white man's spirit and ways. This black Philly nigger had been reformed. He had forgotten what his people had been through; he'd turned his back on them and made his own way.

Albert was constantly on my case. He'd say, "Kelly, who are you trying to fool? You're not tough, you're just a sneaky sly nigger! I'm gonna knock that cool image right out of you!"

In basketball it was war. I'd show him who was king on this court. In roughhouse, we'd fight about points, fouls, and such. He'd try to "Bogart" me, but I'd "Bogart" him right back.

As the season went on we realized we had to work together as a team, and I had a chance to know him better. I was cautious, because down deep I despised Albert and he knew it. But I did begin to see a little what Albert was trying to do.

Then one night we had a school dance. Around 10:00 P.M. I left to get a drink at the store. By the time I returned they had set up refreshments and happened to have the same fruit punch I'd bought. Albert saw me, thought I had filled up my jug with the juice, and ran over with a fist of fury.

I told him, "It's none of your business if I did, so leave me alone." He threw me up against the wall and said, "I know you filled up that container. Why?" I protested: "I went to the store and bought this juice, Buddy, so get out of my face!"

Albert picked up on my threats, getting closer and closer until he was right in my face. That face, that smile, that tone of voice—I just wanted to punch him in the mouth! And Albert knew it. He kept pushing me up the stairs, saying, "Come on, you tough city boy. Hit me right here in the face."

He kept pushing me until finally I did hit him and stunned him. He didn't think I was going to and neither did I. He hit me back, which really stunned me even though I knew it was coming.

Those were the only licks passed in the fight and with that one blow we struck a relationship. He had found out that my "cool" image wasn't really me, and I found out that his concern was genuine. He wasn't an Uncle Tom but a black man who had found himself and what he could do. He had only wanted to share that with me, but first he had to find the real me.

In Albert's mind, the incident at the punch bowl reaffirmed his belief that Kelly was selfish and concerned only about "looking out for number one" rather than sharing with others. Kelly, on the other hand, thought Albert was "on his case," looking for an excuse to badger him because he didn't like him.

Sadly, it was only after their fight that Kelly could finally show his true self to Albert and accept that Albert really was trying to help him. Until that point, Kelly was still controlled by a system that doesn't allow kids—especially males—any other outlet for expressing their love and concern for one another. So they joined cliques in order to feel accepted or learned to hide themselves behind a macho veneer. Only when they were willing to risk everything in a confrontation could they expose their true selves. Perhaps readers can better appreciate why I use the term *desystemize*.

Thanks to Albert's help, Kelly eventually graduated from Hyde School and gained a full academic scholarship to an excellent college.

The Excellence Stage: Spiritual Growth

In the motions stage, students establish the foundation for developing their character and unique potential. In the effort stage they begin to gain some confidence by helping others and reexamining their own attitudes. Finally, they become ready to enter the excellence stage, which requires spiritual growth.

What do we mean by spiritual growth? Something beyond physical, intellectual, and even emotional growth. Something beyond the scope of most American schooling today.

Spiritual growth involves learning to listen to and abide by one's conscience. It means striving to achieve one's loftiest visions and aspirations. It is captured in the desire expressed by students in interviews: to "be the best person I can be," to "help other people," to "leave the world a better place."

Spiritual growth is implicit in the concept of America itself, in the belief that "all men are created equal." It is fostered by embracing the concepts on which America was founded and by discovering in ourselves the spirit of our family heritage.

I never would have believed my own life would end up reflecting the deeper sense of purpose of my stepfather and two great-grandfathers. In rummaging through the attic one day, long after I had discovered my own sense of purpose, I came upon some sermons, apparently written by my maternal great-grandfather, including one on the topic of character development, which he had delivered in Bath, Maine, in 1888! I also read a paper written by my paternal great-grandfather about his Civil War experiences and found myself totally identifying with his deep belief in America. Our heritage is a profound but often hidden part of our own spirit.

Spiritual growth is fostered by living the Five Principles of Destiny, Humility, Conscience, Truth, and Brother's Keeper. It is a lifelong process whose goal of spiritual perfection, like the *daimon* of the Greeks, can be strived for but never fully realized.

Spiritual Growth and the Hyde Diploma

Hyde's role is to inspire spiritual growth in students, provide opportunities for it, and acknowledge it when it occurs. You cannot give away what you don't have; to inspire spiritual growth in students, teachers must themselves develop a deep faith and passion in the concept of unique potential and, ultimately, in America.

Spiritual growth is acknowledged at Hyde by the awarding of a Hyde diploma to any senior who demonstrates that he or she is "ready to conduct his or her life according to standards of personal excellence." Honors signify "exemplary growth" beyond this standard. A certificate is granted for "significant growth"; the student still participates in graduation and is committed to earning a diploma someday but has not yet achieved the diploma standard. A document is granted for meeting Hyde's academic requirements but without "sufficient growth" to warrant participation in graduation.

Awarding diplomas on the basis of growth may seem nebulous to a society accustomed to black-and-white achievement standards such as test scores and grades. But growth, not grades, is the true measure of human development and the best predictor of how a student will fare upon "graduating" into life.

Because we believe that every student has a unique destiny, we give each senior ultimate responsibility for defining what "standards of personal excellence" means to him or her, with the conscience of each individual serving as a guide. In this way we ensure that students become truly self-governing individuals. This is in stark contrast to the system, which places the responsibility for evaluating students in outside hands (teachers, grades, test scores, and such).

The Evaluation Process

Although standards of excellence are determined by individual students, their classmates and teachers participate in the evaluation process. Faculty and seniors meet several times a month during senior year to determine whether each student is truly ready to live up to the standards he or she has set.

Initially seniors may try to control the process. After all, hasn't our achievement emphasis taught them to figure out the surest way to graduate? Isn't it logical for students simply to try to satisfy faculty and classmates' expectations of them? Isn't it frightening even to consider obeying their own consciences instead, risking the disapproval of others and possibly sabotaging their own graduation? But those who trust the process find that obeying one's inner voice generates self-respect and the respect of others.

To trust the process means that students truly consider what they want their lives to be, and what their character ought to be, without rationalizing their shortcomings or overestimating their strengths. It takes courage to trust the evaluation process—which in itself confirms one's character.

Seniors begin evaluations protectively. They fear risking

their relationships by being completely honest in their evaluations of others. They fear that the flaws they find in their fellow classmates may be mirrored in themselves. How can they expect of others what they aren't sure they can expect of themselves?

Seniors find that it's not the evaluation they really fear but the truth of their own consciences. Self-doubts inevitably surface. Students begin to question themselves: "Can I really hear my conscience, much less abide by its dictates?" "Have I truly developed the depth of character necessary to warrant a diploma?" Despite their fears, most seniors find they have invested too much of themselves in Hyde not to give the evaluation process their best shot. If, after an honest examination, they recognize they are not yet ready to live life according to their own standards of excellence, they can simply commit to achieving a diploma later, after spending another year at Hyde or striking out on their own.

The evaluation process requires an enormous amount of time spent in introspection, as seniors take a close inward

look at themselves and their classmates. Yet during the process they continue to attend classes, play on teams, intensely work on the performing arts production for graduation, help juniors assume their leadership role, and still find time to prepare for academic finals. It becomes the most intense experience of their young lives.

Graduating "Clean"

Students sometimes find that their consciences prevent them from graduating because of a past ethical violation they've kept hidden. During the course of evaluations they come to the painful realization that the commitment to standards of excellence, which is symbolized by the Hyde diploma, requires graduating "clean." If they own up to their violations early in the evaluation process, they may still participate in graduation. If not, they will still be certified to go to college, but they'll watch graduation from the audience, learning that respect for one's conscience is more important than disappointing one's family.

My son, Malcolm, writes of his first such experience after he became director of Hyde:

> Mark enrolled in the fall of 1985 after being expelled from a boarding school and professing a desire to turn his life around. But he found the Hyde program very tough, quit once in the first week, thought better of it, and continued. He tried to talk his way through Hyde, and when his peers and teachers pointed out he was "talking the talk but not walking the walk," like a child he stormed off.
>
> But he came back. As tough as the program was, Mark hung in there and slowly earned the respect of others. His academic performance improved. He became a responsible contributor in his dormitory, worked hard in sports, and generally began to talk less and do more.
>
> He entered the evaluation process confidently, stating he felt he deserved a certificate. Both faculty and students concurred. This was a fine achievement, because I can remember only once that a senior who'd been at Hyde for just one year has earned a diploma. We happily regarded Mark as a success story.
>
> But on the day before graduation, during our last evaluation, Mark raised his hand to speak: "Some things have been flying around in my head these past two weeks, and I can't let this process conclude without getting them off my chest. Last September when I was feeling down on myself and Hyde I met some girls in town on a Saturday night. They invited me on a joy ride; we smoked some cigarettes and drank

some vodka. I knew it was wrong, but I rationalized it. Later I justified my behavior as the actions of a new student who didn't understand the importance of Hyde ethics and my role in living up to them.

"But a few weeks ago, when this evaluation process was in full swing, my conscience began bothering me. The honesty in this room is at a depth I have never before experienced. Out of respect for this honesty and my conscience, I cannot accept the Hyde certificate. I am withdrawing my candidacy and I will not participate in the ceremony."

We were stunned. I'd seen this happen before, several times, but this was my maiden voyage as guardian of the process.

Many thoughts went through all our minds in the silence that followed: (1) Raw conscience had just been expressed. (2) No one would otherwise have known of Mark's transgression. (3) He had clearly violated the student ethic and had earlier ignored his chance to "clear the decks" and graduate "clean." (4) Since he was exemplifying the purpose of the evaluation, how could we penalize him?

I finally broke the silence by asking Mark if he was sure of his decision. (I was really stalling.) He indicated he was. Nevertheless, I suggested he give it twenty-four hours of thought. A discussion ensued, and a split opinion emerged from the living room of the Mansion.

Mark didn't participate in graduation; he sat in the audience with his family. I'm not sure his parents truly understood, but we held him in the highest respect. Afterward, he congratulated his classmates and clearly was not asking for pity.

Underclassmen seemed baffled, but Mark left them a legacy on the sanctity of the process they would later experience in a way that none of my words could. Mark was once considered a talker, but now his deeds more than matched his words.

Today Mark is doing well at a selective Eastern college and plans to return for his diploma some day.

He's visited several times, and we've spoken on the phone. He is proud of his year at Hyde, and we are proud of him.

"Fools Never Change, But Men Do"

Sometimes the final decision about graduation comes down to the last minute, which may make the process seem heartless to outsiders. I remember how the K.s, one of our first black families, struggled with this evaluation process with their first two sons. Joanne, the younger sister, writes:

> In 1969 my oldest brother left Hyde School during his last term. Unable to make the commitment to attaining his best, he ran from the discovery of his unique potential. Because of this disappointment, our family looked forward to my brother Harold's commencement five years later, signifying a dream and a hope of my mother.
>
> But when my family and friends arrived, Harold told them he and his classmates had decided he was not ready to graduate. Although they knew of the Hyde requirements, my family didn't truly understand that academic achievements don't prepare one to lead one's life by rigorous standards of excellence, or to continue striving for the fulfillment of one's own unique potential.
>
> My family and friends cried tears that were so painful; Harold looked devastated, although he understood. We all stayed through graduation, because Harold and I wanted to be there when our friends graduated. However, my grandfather was extremely upset and said he would not attend my graduation next year or ever set foot on the Hyde campus again.
>
> I returned to Hyde for my senior year, while Harold ventured out on his own to prove to himself that he could live his life by standards of excellence. Harold struggled with many things; but by the end of the year he felt he was ready to graduate and returned to Hyde to discuss his progress and to be evaluated by the faculty, my classmates, and the headmaster.

The K.s lived in a white neighborhood. I believe their struggles were rooted in a spiritual conflict of trying to become part of a community with at least unconscious prejudices, while trying to remain true to their own heritage and spirit. The mother will almost instinctively protect her family from hurt in such cases; Harold's year on his own was necessary to confront the protection.

Joanne continues:

> On graduation morning 1975 Harold and I graduated from Hyde School together, an experience I can't describe in words. One amazing thing did happen. I wrote to my grandfather, trying to make him understand and telling him why he should come to graduation. He wrote back: "I will be there; fools never change, but men do."

Harold went on to graduate from Bowdoin and today is the chief admissions officer at a leading university. Joanne graduated from Wellesley College and became a labor relations administrator. But in 1988 she followed her heart and joined the Hyde faculty.

Working through the Stages: Ann's Story

Ann Adams applied to Hyde School for her senior year. The Adamses were a solid, conscientious American family living in a wealthy suburb. Both parents were college graduates. The family attended church regularly and were active in community affairs; Mr. Adams was chairman of the school board. The Adamses held high standards for their five children.

Ann carried on in the family tradition: her IQ tests placed her in the top 1 percent of her peers; she had achieved high honors in each grade and had won a national honor in Latin. When Ann applied to Hyde, her previous school rated her "high to exceptional" in personal responsibility, consideration for others, depth of understanding, involvement, and evenness of performance. Ann's recommendations showed that her teachers were completely satisfied with her: "Ann is a very independent person who responds well to challenges.

. . ." "A very happy, well-adjusted girl—well liked by her peers and teachers." "We all regret losing Ann, a very able student and a very warm person."

But underneath this veneer of perfection, Ann was a deeply troubled youngster who was heavily involved in drugs and sex. Ann had simply pretended to be what adults wanted her to be, because in her words, "things went so much more smoothly" when she did so. Drugs and sex were a way of temporarily numbing the pain she felt over having to hide her true self, of not being able to discuss her valid adolescent problems and concerns with her parents and teachers.

Eventually Ann's parents discovered the truth, and after an explosive confrontation, the family decided to apply to Hyde. The soul-searching admissions interview helped them all go through a painful examination of themselves, their deeper values, their attitudes, and what they truly wanted to accomplish in their lives. Once they agreed on the need to change, Ann began the six-week Summer Challenge program and underwent our process of desystemization. Ann's parents also began participating in our Family Learning Center, which I'll discuss in Chapter 7.

Ann writes:

> I was scared to death of Hyde at first. It took me awhile to begin to adjust and to really trust and bank on what the school was saying.
>
> I began building this trust when I finally turned myself in for doing speed my first week at Hyde. This was a huge step for me. Never before had I, a girl so pushed toward achievement that it wasn't funny, deliberately blown the whistle on myself. I did it because I didn't feel I was getting everything I could out of Hyde.
>
> I immediately felt the lightheartedness of getting a burden off my shoulders. People, especially faculty members, were shocked and disappointed in me, but I felt clean—honest, like I at least had some solid ground to build on.
>
> Pleasing people, being liked—these have always been so important to me. There's such a difference

between feeling that others like me and liking myself, though.

I was kind of sad at disappointing Mr. Kent [one of her teachers], but at least I forced him to take a look at me as I really was. When I went before the students and faculty who would decide my "punishment," I felt the same way—very straightforward.

I wanted to do something hard to prove my will to change. Strange as it sounds, I was glad to get up at five or six in the morning and go out and pull weeds around the duck pond. I really felt honest.

At this point Ann was making a rapid transition away from the system and into the Hyde concept, even though she was an older student (seventeen at the time). She confronted her dependency on achievement and image by turning herself in for taking drugs. And she began to put her faith in the truth and ultimately in her own unique potential.

Ann went on to have a fine year at Hyde, graduating with a diploma that implied she was ready to live her life up to her own standards of excellence. But her pace turned out to be too rapid. She writes: "Today I graduated from Hyde. I'm fairly sure I want and need to come back to Hyde next year, but Mother is having a hard time trying to understand this. I feel very hopeful, though, about where I am and what I can help her understand about me during the coming summer."

I thought Ann really did need another year at Hyde to achieve her best growth. Her summer on her own turned out to be rather unproductive. She was still dependent on her parents. And although she had decided to attend college, she was actually more interested in getting on the success treadmill than in using college as a tool to help her find herself. At the end of the summer, Ann came back to Hyde and discussed her situation. She tearfully agreed that she was not yet ready to live life by her own standards of excellence. To her credit, she returned her diploma.

Ann ultimately decided to live on her own. We had a long talk one evening that fall, and the next morning I found this letter in my box:

Dear Mr. Gauld,

I'm leaving early tomorrow morning; I have to get back to work. I plan to take a very deep and serious look at where I am, and where my life is, during the coming days and weeks. I plan to write a commitment paper for myself about what I'm going to do in order to earn my Hyde School diploma. I also hope my writing will find that core on which I can build.

I'll be in touch with you real soon. Thank you for your concern—it's really important to me to know you care.

I love you,
Ann

More than a year later, in 1976, Ann wrote again:

I got a Christmas card today from a customer at the restaurant where I worked last year—someone whose name I didn't even know. At first I felt plain surprise. Later, I felt both very happy and sad because it struck me that someone, in thinking of Christmas, remembered the counter girl.

That's me—me without the strings and dependencies. Me living my life, not anyone else's idea of what my life should be. Working on my own, I have felt more self-reliant and independent than ever before.

I had to break away. No one can give you your independence; you've got to fight for it. I've managed to miss the idea of this Bicentennial all year long, and it's just now hit me that that's what America did. Fought for her independence and won. That's America's spirit and what the people of this country should be. . . . This last paragraph is where I stopped writing last night and started thinking. About so many things! Thank you so much for being part of my life. I can't explain it, but a feeling came over me of commitment, of wanting to change the world, a strong desire to fight for something better. . . .

I said a prayer—something I haven't done in a long

time. . . . For once I wasn't saying help me . . . , or please take care of so-and-so. I just asked Him to be with me as I tried to do some good. It's a whole new idea to me and it excites me.

I'll write you again soon—thanks for calling me and getting me started.

Much love,
Ann

By rejecting her parents' advice to go to college and our advice to return to Hyde, Ann made the best decision for herself; for students brought up in sheltered environments, living and working outside the gates often brings a new reality to Hyde lessons. In spite of the fact that she was then just eighteen years old, Ann had accomplished an important step in letting go of adolescence and entering adulthood.

Ann's writing describes the complete cycle of growth: her motions stage in summer school; her effort stage, in which she begins to take responsibility for her life but still needs more help; and, finally, the excellence stage, when she finds she can really trust the deeper values of her family and her own spirit and wants to change the world.

Ann's transformation was not a flash in the pan. She went on to college, did postgraduate work, and today has two wonderful children and an exemplary career in nursing administration.

Hyde is a fine school, but no school can create this magic. Half of Ann's transformation occurred in a restaurant in the city! The credit goes to Ann's spirit and to the strong foundation of values and character provided by her family— the most powerful determinant in the character–unique potential concept.

CHAPTER 5

Family:
A New Frontier

Just as the twig is bent the tree's inclined.
—Alexander Pope

en came from a wealthy Chicago suburb. He was admittedly spoiled and doing badly in school but claimed he was now ready "to put my mind to full capacity to do my best." His counselor agreed: "[Len] comes from a home that has offered him everything physically . . . he has potential, and if placed in the proper environment, will be a credit to any institution." His parents vowed to stop making things easy for Len and to do whatever was necessary to draw out the best in him.

Len made a good start at Hyde, but then he began to slip. Accustomed to being coddled, he eventually decided that Hyde was too much of a hassle for him and that he wanted to leave. At the admissions interview I had warned both Len and his parents of this possibility: "I know you and Len are sure he won't throw in the towel, Mr. L., but just suppose he does?" Mr. L. had agreed that he would not allow Len to come home.

Now, as Len and I sat in my office, with his father on the speaker telephone, Mr. L.'s voice on the line was strong. He reminded Len of their mutual commitment: either Len would stay at Hyde or go out on his own. Len looked at me and smiled. "He doesn't mean it." Stunned, Mr. L. shot back, "Len, no human being is going to run over me like this, not even my own son!"

Len did leave school; and, as usual, the child knew the parent. In less than three weeks his father relented and allowed Len to come home.

Mr. L. initially refused to let his son in when he showed up on his doorstep. So Len went to live with friends, and Mr. L. called me every day for advice. He naturally worried about Len being on his own, as would the parents of any sixteen-year-old boy. But as I told him, "that's the price of preparing a child for life with words and not with deeds." I added: "As time goes on, the price will become higher. It's as if Len is on an elevator going up, and he must get off. If he jumps now, he will only get bloody. If he waits, it might be too late."

In the end, the son won. His father rationalized his decision to let Len come home: "Joe, my name is mud with all the neighbors," and later, "Joe, I have no choice. If I don't let him back, my wife will end up in a basket." I warned him of the lives I'd seen lost to hospitals, jails, even suicide, when parents didn't stand fast—but to no avail.

Six years later I wrote a column on runaways and called Mr. L. He told me the sequel: After leaving Hyde and coming home, Len fell into a pattern of running away periodically. Then came psychiatric help and hospitals. Mr. L. and his wife eventually divorced, primarily over Len's problems. By the time he was nineteen, Len was institutionalized. Six weeks before my call he had killed a fellow patient.

"What now?" I asked. Mr. L. thought Len would be judged innocent by reason of insanity, but he added that his son had been "babied and coddled enough" and vowed that he would not put Len in "another plush hospital." This time, in the state hospital, "he would have to work his way out." I wanted to say, "What you do speaks so loudly, I can't hear what you say," but I knew my comment would fall on deaf ears.

The Spiritual Decline of the American Family

The family has traditionally been the foundation of American education, with parents instilling in their children the American values of hard work, character, and a deeper sense of purpose. But over the course of my forty-two years of teaching I have witnessed a continual disintegration of these values. Personally, I have never seen youngsters as confused about who they are, as lacking in a sense of their ultimate purpose in life, as are today's youth.

Having worked intimately with thousands of families, I have come to an inescapable conclusion: The American family today is spiritually sick. It is increasingly being fractured by a new brand of American individualism that appeals to our selfish side rather than drawing out our unique potential.

Mr. L. is a prime example of the spiritually sick parent. Although he claims to want what is best for his son, when a crisis arises he worries, not about his son's character development or future, but about what the neighbors will think and about his wife's problems. He no doubt feels guilty for failing

Len, but he is willing to help him only if doing so doesn't upset his own comfortable life-style.

To parents like the L.s the American dream never goes beyond the fulfillment of their own superficial desires for material acquisitions and the good life. Questions of character and a deeper sense of purpose, if they are addressed at all, are reduced to intellectual concerns and are never integrated into their daily lives. Such parents may preach the importance of deeper values to their children, but as Len's story points out, children usually pay attention only to actions; words alone mean nothing.

The upbringing of kids like Len leaves them totally unprepared for life, both spiritually and materially. Even though they are led to believe they have everything, they have been taught to expect nothing of themselves. Their lives are empty, devoid of meaning. This helps to explain the alarmingly high rates of crime and suicide among affluent suburban teenagers.

Matt's Story

Len's story has been repeated many times at Hyde. Because the school is financially dependent on tuition income, the majority of candidates come from affluent suburbia. Some of these kids are unable to trade the easy suburban life-style for the deeper values of Hyde, and they opt to leave the school. Matt was one of them.

Matt began Hyde in the summer of 1967. He'd had problems in school and at home; but he was academically bright, scoring at the ninety-ninth percentile on achievement tests. Matt's divorced parents were caught up in their affluent life-styles and had failed to provide any direction for their son. The father was preoccupied with his business and with maintaining his image of success. The mother was so preoccupied with her own problems that she couldn't be of much help to Matt.

Although Matt had a promising first year at Hyde, I was unable to win his commitment to return for a second year. Not surprisingly, he chose the glamour and independence his father's life-style seemed to offer over what Hyde said he needed.

I told Matt he'd never make it on his own and made him write a commitment paper about what he would do once he was back in public school. I hoped that he would one day read what he had written, recognize the truth of his situation, and return to Hyde. Here is some of what Matt wrote:

> As a high school freshman I was in a state of existence seldom seen by teenagers anywhere except perhaps in the worst of slums.
>
> I was never short of money so most of my wishes came true. But I was uncaring, completely irresponsible, and irrational. I stole cars, boats, anything returnable. (For some reason I always returned what I stole, maybe through some remnant of childhood conditioning.)
>
> Using my fists gave me great pleasure; it still does. But in the past I took a savage joy in crushing someone's face whereas now I use my fists as a sport.
>
> I used to think, "Why should I live? I don't want money; money's nothing. I don't want parents. All parents do is fight, throw things, get separated, scream on the telephone, and bring me to court for a divorce case." I used to wonder, "What does the future hold for me?"
>
> But since coming to Hyde my outlook on life has almost completely changed. I now look forward to the future; there is so much to live for. I have goals—a good job, one that I like; a good life; and a reasonably contented death.
>
> That is the biggest change Hyde has made in me. Study habits, academics, and the school's values have only left a slight impression on me, but for this one basic change in my character, I thank Hyde School.
>
> Contrary to public opinion, I know I won't go down the drain in public school. At home I'll have a chance to really work on my hobbies, deeply commit myself to boxing, cars, reading good literature, keep out of the

cops' way, keep my marks up, and generally lead an outwardly straight, fun life.

I need a free, unrestricted life where I can make my own rules and don't have to bother with petty foolishness like lights-out, mandatory meals, and campus restrictions. Without these aggravations, I'll be able to do my homework with complete concentration. Soon I'll be put to the test; soon it will be seen who is right—you or me. I'll be back next year with my report card.

Matt's story reflects the spiritual sickness inherent in the suburban emphasis on money and position, and the lack of deeper values. Matt has no concept of a purpose beyond himself. His perception is so limited that he believes Hyde has changed his "character," while at the same time admitting that Hyde's values left only a "slight impression" on him and referring to our character-building rules as "petty foolishness"! In fact, Matt left Hyde as he came—with only a superficial understanding of life and a total lack of a spiritual foundation.

Matt did visit me the following year. By then he had dropped out of school, and without his parents' support I couldn't get him to make the commitment to return to Hyde. Matt eventually drifted into crime. In 1975 he was murdered, apparently in a gang fight.

"Fix-It" Parents

As Hyde encountered more and more kids who resisted dealing with their problems, I became increasingly aware of the same resistance in their parents. Parents would often come to us in desperation over their out-of-control son or daughter. Even though they pledged their commitment to bringing out the best in themselves (knowing this was a condition of their child's admission to Hyde), they clearly expressed their belief that the child's problems had nothing to do with their own. Their philosophy was, Here's a kid who isn't working right; we'll pay you to fix him up and send him back to us. We came to refer to them as "fix-it" parents.

As terrible as it sounds, I have sensed in such parents the feeling that if somehow their child were accidentally killed, their deep remorse would be mixed with relief and a feeling of vindication. At least their parenting skills couldn't be called into question.

After a while the progress of their sons and daughters exposed the real source of the problem: the parents. Instead of being pleased when their children began developing character and adopting deeper values, fix-it parents often became personally threatened and in some cases withdrew their support of the school. In other cases, Hyde would help the son or daughter make dramatic progress in a short period of time, only to have the parents feel the kid was now cured and our school was no longer necessary. Even when the truth of the family's deeper problems came crashing down later, as it did in Matt's case, the parents often remained impervious to it.

Lost in the Suburban Ghetto

In many ways Matt was a sensitive kid with great potential, but his parents' lesser values were so deeply ingrained in him that Hyde was a case of too little, too late. Len and Matt are dramatic, but not exceptional, examples of the spiritual poverty of the suburban ghetto. Bart is still another example.

Bart came to Hyde after being arrested as the ringleader of a gang of well-off suburban kids who were involved in breaking into homes and committing major thefts. A year after he arrived at Hyde, he made a major step by writing the following paper, in which he identifies the spiritual corruption in his family and begins to accept responsibility for changing his life:

> Ever since I can remember, my father always came home from work at seven, made himself a drink, and read the newspaper while he talked with my mother about the day as she made dinner. We were always afraid to go into the kitchen then, because Dad was always "tired" and didn't want us to bother him.
>
> He would often work on Saturdays, and on the weekends when he didn't, he'd be in his workshop, or

watching a football game—generally relaxing. On Sundays he played golf.

Considering that my father was never around, I don't know why I didn't get closer to my mother. Maybe because she never messed around with us.

During my father's nightly two-hour lectures on how I should grow up I used to get mad and stick up for myself, but I always lost. My mother would say "Shut up" to me under her breath, because when I disagreed we'd end up in a fight, and I'd get sent to bed, or occasionally we'd get violent.

Finally I realized what a fool I was, and I just shut up the whole time. When asked a question, I'd give the desired response.

I finally got to the point where if I wasn't allowed to go out, I'd just get into a fight with my father and get him to kick me out of the house. I could usually do it in twenty minutes or so.

I remember once I wanted to be at a friend's house at nine o'clock. At eight-thirty I walked into the kitchen and my father started lecturing me. I didn't say a word until five of nine, when I sighed. He was already mad, so he picked up four glasses and threw them at me, smashing them against the wall right next to my face. I got mad, but I controlled myself enough to just leave. My mother, of course, cleaned up the mess, and the other kids just listened from the other room, scared.

I remember another time when I was a little younger, when my father was lecturing me during dinner, with everyone there at the table. My mother kept saying little things, telling him to calm down and stuff, but my father just got madder. He said if she said one more thing he'd pick up the table and throw it on top of her.

She did, and he picked up his end of the table and spilled all the food and milk and dishes all over everybody. The little kids and my mother were crying—everybody except Dad, who was just mad at everybody.

You see on TV the husband who comes home drunk every night, beats his wife and all the kids, and the story of the family is that their lives are hell. They don't have much money, they live in the slums, and so on. If we had lived in the slums, I might have had a better idea of how to cope with it, but we've always been very affluent, which has just blinded me to the whole situation.

I don't want my youngest and favorite sister to grow up in that family. I'm scared to death she'll turn out like me and my brothers. Even my thirteen-year-old sister is starting to go that way.

I want to get myself established somewhere, with some kind of income, and take her and bring her up myself until she's old enough to manage. I know she won't have all of the things my father can give her, but I can give her things he can't buy. As it is now, she'll grow up without that sense of being needed. Pretty soon Dad's "Santa Claus" role will be gone, and there won't be anything to replace it.

I have never felt important to, or needed by, my parents. I know they love me, and I figure I must be important in their lives, but I arrive at that by logic; I never actually felt it. It makes me feel incomplete, like I just don't have some basic human character everyone else does. I always feel I've missed out on something really important.

I love my parents, but only because they are my parents, biologically. I do not know either of them beyond that. My image of them is one of perfection. My father stands for excellence, very high moral standards, and he is a genius, while my mother is pretty smart too and stands for exactly the same values.

The only time I could ever cry over my parents is when I think what I am missing. I envy others whom I see hug their parents and talk with them. But I have to make do with what I have. I just want to get away from them, because for me they are ropes that bind me.

Everything always happened to me or was done for me. I never was given the freedom to live, to make

> anything happen by myself. I want to do something by myself, without my parents behind me, without Hyde to save me—even to fail miserably at something. I've been a big boy for several years now, but I've never had a chance to make anything happen for myself.
>
> The only way that I can grow up is to divorce myself from my parents. I will not come back here next year if my parents pay for it. I'll have to work out something for myself.

Bart's father is a highly successful executive, yet he has no relationship with his children. His leadership is reduced to childish tantrums when his family doesn't respond to his directives. It measures our sickness today that a parent can fail so miserably with his family and still be considered an outstanding success in the eyes of our society. Even Bart, who has been the victim of his father's outrageous behavior, has been seduced into holding an image of his parents as "perfect"!

Except for extreme abuse or neglect, there are no standards for American parenting. Americans won't let some drugstore cowboy hang out a shingle to practice law or medicine, but we will let parents raise American kids any way they please. And then we try to clean up their messes in our schools, hospitals, courtrooms, and jails.

When we confronted Bart's father regarding his attitudes, his commitment to Hyde collapsed and he withdrew his family from the Hyde community. At least Bart acted on his desire to "do something by myself"; he left home and supported himself while going to college. I later heard that his father was in court, trying to disown another son. Yet our courts still haven't demanded one shred of accountability from *him*.

Where Is Mom?

You may have noticed there is a missing player in each of these stories: Mom. We would expect the mothers of these kids to be out in front, fighting for their children's future. But during Matt's crisis, his mother was lost in her own problems. Len's mother's instability killed her son's last chance for a future ("My wife will end up in a basket"). Bart's mother tried to placate her husband rather than stand up for her son, instead pleading with Bart, under her breath, to shut up in order to avoid a fight. When she does try to calm down the irate dad, he responds by dumping the kitchen table, filled with food and dishes, on her. She cries, but nothing changes.

Mom must stand for something, insist that her children and husband respect deeper values, and then help guide the family to live by those values. For the American mother is the true and natural leader of the family and, as the real power behind the throne, the leader of our society as well.

This powerful statement may express a personal bias, since I consider my own mother the core of my growth and my wife the core of our children's growth and essential in the realization of my own unique potential. But my extensive experience with American families validates this bias and compels me to make this observation.

A committed father might take over this critical role of the mother—like an artificial heart. But so far I have noted significant problems in such transformations. Perhaps there is a biological basis for these problems. After all, the mother carries the child for nine months and goes through the profound experience of childbirth, in all its joy and pain. The father, on the other hand, need not participate in the process at all, beyond conception. Because of this, the father simply may not experience the deep level of bonding with his child that the mother does.

The Family's Spiritual Leader

I believe the spiritual leadership of a family begins with the mother—a designation that assumes she has already significantly matured in both her girl and woman stages, as my wife had when we married.

I met Blanche on a blind date in high school. After splitting up several times, we drifted closer to marriage. (She finally had to ask in exasperation, "Are we going to get married?") I was very immature, but I think we had a spiritual attraction beyond our egos.

Blanche grew up faster than I did, probably through the deeper truths of her farm upbringing and the tough challenges

her family faced, including the loss of her father and two brothers during World War II. She was a very mature teenager and assumed womanhood with ease. But I was immature, still a boy at heart. In many ways I viewed Blanche somewhat like a mother; thank God, she was woman enough not to take control of me during my vulnerable period. She never hesitated regarding my desire to try teaching even though the lack of privacy of boarding school life went against her grain. She accepted this life of anticipated poverty—my first job paid $1,800 a year—because she sensed my ability with kids.

Better still, she expected me to be a man. After losing my first two games as head football coach, I was called to a meeting where I knew the administration would ask me to change my offense. I fumed to Blanche, "I'll quit first!" (expecting her to "mother" me and give me an excuse to give in). I was stunned when she actually took the suitcases down from the closet shelf! (She later admitted she had felt I was too accommodating and needed to stand up for myself. But she said absolutely nothing at the time.)

So I didn't back down. Incredibly, they did. I made my offense work—and became both a football coach and a man. But I had needed Blanche's character and her confidence in me to stand my ground.

Children also need the confidence and character modeling that mothers provide. Mothers tend to emphasize the inner development of family members, and fathers, their outer relationship to life. So the mother's leadership nurtures and protects the children's unique potential from undue outside pressures. By the time they become adults they have developed a strong sense of themselves, which enables them to resist pressure from the outside world to conform to images or adopt behaviors that are not true to their inner selves.

Reasserting the Leadership Role: Mrs. D.'s Story

Unfortunately, American business in general, and especially the large corporation, pressures the executive who is also a father to ignore rather than develop a sense of commitment to his family. (The same pressure is now being applied to the growing number of female executives.) Under this pressure the inner spiritual leadership represented by the mother often gives way to the outer, ego-orientation of the father, with tragic results, as we noted in the stories of Len, Matt, and Bart.

Mrs. D., a Hyde mother, writes of her own struggle to stand up to her husband's ego and reassert her role as the spiritual leader of the family:

> All I've ever wanted to be was a mother, yet now that I've started to listen to a little voice inside, I realize the two biggest mistakes I've made in my life may kill my son Danny. My first mistake was in not marrying a man who would be a real father for my children; the second was in consciously choosing to stay with him.

Because my parents' lives were in such a mess, I married a man unlike my father. I was attracted by John's sense of responsibility, his aggressive ambition, his self-discipline, and his serious approach to life. I could also see his more sensitive side, which he tried to keep hidden. The romantic in me proclaimed this the perfect marriage—I'd married Heathcliff, and only my bright, optimistic, and undying love would bring out his warmth and tenderness.

But the qualities in John's character I'd admired so much soon became a burden. Deciding the trouble must be in me, I was determined to start growing up and stop being the butterfly.

Soon I found myself deeply enmeshed in a trap of my own making: emotionally and financially dependent, with too little confidence in my own beliefs. But I continued to go along with John, telling myself I could and would change him.

Then my father died. After the initial shock I told John I was going to take the two babies and fly home for the funeral. His response was as big a shock as my father's death. He told me that I couldn't manage the trip by myself; he asked who would take care of our upcoming move, and he said we couldn't afford the plane fare.

My tears and arguments didn't make a dent, and I ended up once again giving in. At the time I couldn't forgive John; now I realize I can't forgive myself for selling out on something so important.

That capitulation was the big step down the wrong road for all of us. I kidded myself into believing that going home for the funeral wasn't important. I also told myself that, with renewed determination, I could make John understand my point of view and accept some of my values that I thought were important for the family. We had two more children, and I continued to live with dissatisfaction and compromise, feeling "this, too, shall pass," while a little voice inside me kept saying, "the children, the children . . ."

It was Danny who finally got through to me. He was
such a strange combination: noisy, laughing, and full
of mischief, and yet often so paralyzed that he wouldn't
try new things because he was so afraid of failure.
Most of his school days were spent in daydreams.

Although I'd listened for years to how John had
changed from a dullard in grammar school to a
budding genius in junior high, I knew by the time
Danny was in eighth grade that he needed help. He
was already a sneak and a liar and was becoming a
bully. What had happened to all of our preaching that
honest, industrious, clean living brought success in
life? I can still remember with chagrin my lofty
lectures and noble-sounding advice. But it obviously
wasn't working.

I found Hyde School by accident. During most of the
three-hour interview, I was more scared than Danny,
because I realized what the stakes were. I don't
remember much that was said in the interview, because
I kept saying to myself, "Please, God, don't let John be
spooked off."

By the end of summer school, the positive changes in
Danny were evident to us: he was more confident and
responsible, a little braver and more eager, and had a
new maturity and ability to understand himself.

After a successful freshman year, Danny went to
work in a boatyard (one of John's investments). Then
John decided that Danny and his brother should go
into the lobstering business.

Although both boys protested vigorously, John wore
them down, and finally the irresistible bait of having
their own boat did them in. All during the campaign,
John ignored me, insisting that any boy would just
love doing this work; after all, hadn't he?

Danny's working hours kept expanding, as did his
original financial involvement, until he finally just
stopped going to work and lied about it. The next
several weeks were a mixture of confrontations,
ultimatums, Danny leaving and coming home again,

with all of us holding our collective breaths as we slowly slipped back into our pre-Hyde ways.

Then the inevitable happened. With no room left for persuasion, intimidation, bribery, or whatever other weapons Danny faced in the uneven battle with his father over how his life was to be lived, he ran away. And I began to hear that little voice inside me.

John and I accepted Mr. Gauld's advice: let Danny choose to go back to Hyde or go out on his own. But John became more worried and upset as the weeks passed. Danny's bankbook disappeared from our house, and withdrawals had been made, so we knew he was back in town. I knew his younger brother was reporting daily to Danny on the weakening of his father's resolve, although he denied it. Finally, after two weeks of no word from Danny, John really fell apart. He announced at dinner that he'd had enough, he'd made up his mind, and was going to bring Danny home.

Before he could carry out his decision Danny came home—in a police cruiser. He had been caught with others smoking pot in a shack in the woods. The police told me that if I took him home, there wouldn't be any charges. I could see the officer mentally shaking his head when I told him I couldn't. Danny left for a night in the local jail, and I sat down to wait for my husband.

John was horrified that I'd let my own son be arrested. How could a mother deny her own son the love and loyalty of his family in this, his darkest hour? After spending two hours with a lawyer, John returned home full of confidence, determined that "no school is going to tell me how to raise my child."

The lawyer advised John that I should go to court the next morning and tell Danny he had the choice of either going back to Hyde or being sent to a detention center. However, if he chose the detention center, I was simply to bring him home!

I could see how firmly Danny was caught in an extremely negative pattern. We'd been letting him manipulate us for so many years, playing one parent against the other with his emotional blackmail, that we'd raised a fifteen-year-old con artist with the emotional maturity of a six-year-old. If these mistakes didn't stop now, I knew he wouldn't have any chance at all.

I told John that I totally disagreed with the lawyer's advice. I said I would leave the house myself rather than take Danny home, to give him a real choice.

I guess John didn't believe me. He sent me off to court with the same instructions, probably feeling he could convince us all that night that we could live happily ever after.

At the police station I told Danny what his choices actually were: he could return to Hyde School, or his father would take him home. I told him why I was leaving (to give him a choice), and that it might very well be too late for him to change, but it was the only chance he had. You can spend years telling your kids what's right and wrong, but what they really understand is how you actually live your life.

Danny chose to live with his father and to go to a local high school—exactly what he'd wanted to do two months earlier when we'd told him the choice was either Hyde or to live on his own. He and his father settled in to develop an "honest relationship" based on mutual trust and responsibility. My daughter continued at Hyde, and I took the other two children to live with me.

Within three months Danny had been arrested in two states for breaking and entering and car theft. He had also stolen some jewelry left to his sister by her grandmother and had three or four brief episodes of running away. All I can do now is make sure the option stays open if Danny wants help in growing up.

Many years later I received a letter from Mrs. D.'s daughter. She wrote:

> If there is one skill I gained from my time at Hyde for which I am most grateful, it is that I learned (oddly in a high school) how to be a good parent. In raising my own children (two daughters), I frequently find myself calling upon those values I learned to embrace while at Hyde—and it works! I must also strongly assert that the role model I was lucky enough to have for motherhood was a strong and sensitive woman. I watched her parent—often well, sometimes making mistakes, but always growing and facing life's struggles with courage and life's pleasures with joy. I have the utmost respect for her.

As I read the letter from Mrs. D.'s daughter, I came back again and again to the words her mother had written earlier: "You can spend years telling your kids what's right and wrong, but what they really understand is how you actually live your life." Mrs. D.'s courage has had a profound impact on her daughter's life, and it may someday save the lives of her other children—if they find the courage and faith to follow her.

Parent, Heal Thyself

The kids in this chapter were all reachable; it was the parents we couldn't reach. Accordingly, because we were unable to win over the parents, we ultimately couldn't reach their children.

Parents are the primary teachers of children, and the home is the primary classroom. No matter how dismal their backgrounds, when their parents genuinely commit themselves to the unique-potential concept, children invariably succeed, at Hyde and later in life. Without such parental commitment, most Hyde students fail to realize their potential, no matter how great our initial success with them.

This was a painful reality for me to accept. When I founded Hyde I believed that we could reach any kid. But over time I was forced to conclude that, in the long run, our best efforts with students like Len, Matt, and Bart could seldom overcome the worst in their families. I came to understand that if Hyde wanted to contribute to reversing the steady decline in American education, we first had to address the problems of American families.

CHAPTER 6

The Need for Healthy Parenting

Your children are not your children,
They are the sons and daughters of Life's longing for itself.
They come through you but not from you,
And though they are with you yet they belong not to you.

You may give them your love but not your thoughts,
For they have their own thoughts.
You may house their bodies but not their souls,
For their souls dwell in the house of tomorrow,
    which you cannot visit, not even in your dreams.
You may strive to be like them,
    but seek not to make them like you.
For life goes not backward nor tarries with yesterday.

You are the bows from which your children as living
    arrows are sent forth.
The Archer sees the mark upon the path of the infinite,
And He bends you with His might that His arrows may go
    swift and far.
Let your bending in the Archer's hand be for gladness;
For even as He loves the arrow that flies,
So He loves also the bow that is stable.
                                    —Kahlil Gibran, *The Prophet*

P arenting and teaching have taught me the deepest reverence for the wisdom of Gibran's words. Although children begin life totally dependent upon us, Gibran reminds us that we do not own them; we are merely assistants to a power greater than ourselves. We must resist raising our children in our own image, for the purpose of their lives is beyond our comprehension.

This can be an ego-deflating realization for dedicated parents, but it is also liberating. It means we are not ultimately responsible for our children's destinies; all we are required to do is our best. And whatever our parenting problems, help is always available from this greater power who loves us as "the bow that is stable."

The Lesson of Abraham

The Bible states that children are born "not of blood, nor of the will of the flesh, nor of the will of the man, but of God." In Genesis, God tells Abraham to make a burnt sacrifice of his only son, Isaac. Abraham dutifully goes to the appointed place, binds his son, places him on the sacrificial altar, and raises his knife to plunge it into Isaac's heart. At the last moment, God prevents Abraham from inflicting the fatal wound and tells him, "Because you have done this, and have not withheld your only son, I will indeed bless you and I will multiply your descendants as the stars in heaven. . . ."

Americans have difficulty with this story because we see Isaac as *Abraham's* child, not God's. By giving our children our very best, we consider them to be a part of ourselves. But Abraham accepted with his heart, body, and soul that Isaac was *God's* child, and that God's wisdom and purpose for the child was beyond his understanding; his job was simply to have faith.

When I was growing up, stories like this made me reject the Bible as a serious source of wisdom. What kind of wimp

The Prophet (New York: Alfred A. Knopf, 1973), pp. 17–18. Copyright 1923 by Kahlil Gibran and renewed 1951 by Administrators C.T.A. of Kahlil Gibran Estate and Mary G. Gibran. Reprinted by permission of Alfred A. Knopf, Inc.

117

or monster would kill his only child for anyone, much less for a cruel God's celebration? But age has taught me the deeper wisdom of this biblical tale: if we are able to "let go" of our children and trust in a higher power to assist us in raising them, we will have a profound influence on future generations.

As a youth, I never would have believed that my own life would eventually reflect the attitudes and convictions of my two great-grandfathers. Although they lived more than 100 years ago, their commitment to character development and their strong belief in America have been passed down through the generations. Our egos die with us, but the truth of our conscience lives on.

The Spiritual Parent

The humility of Abraham is clearly a spiritual quality, which leads to my definition of the spiritual parent: one who humbly accepts that his or her child has a purpose and a destiny dictated by a higher power. Let me illustrate:

Suppose your fifteen-year-old son skins his knee, and with time the wound unaccountably becomes worse. The doctor, after extensive treatment, finds that the wound has gangrene and reluctantly recommends amputation. You call in a specialist from another city who confirms the tragic diagnosis. You finally muster the courage to tell your son that he must have the operation because the alternative is death. He refuses, saying, "I'd rather be dead than crippled and unable to play ball." What do you do?

In fact, this scenario is based on a true account of the life of Dwight Eisenhower. At age fifteen Eisenhower was faced with such a life-threatening wound and argued against amputation so that he could continue to play football. Although his parents were against contact sports, they acknowledged their son's right to make such a decision and sorrowfully accepted his. Obviously, his decision turned out to be right, as he made a miraculous recovery.

When I first read Ike's account of this episode, I was curious to see how my wife, Blanche, would react, because I considered her to be a spiritual parent. I asked what she would do if the same thing were to happen to our son Malcolm at fifteen and got this exchange:

"I would check with other doctors," she replied.

"Suppose they agreed?"

"Well . . . then I would talk to Malcolm."

"But suppose he still balked?"

"Well . . . we'd talk some more."

"Blanche, I know you're confident that you could eventually bring Malcolm around but suppose you couldn't?"

After a long pause she said, "It would kill me, but I guess I would have to go along with his refusal."

I expected this answer from Blanche, who ultimately accepted that such a decision would be between her son and his God. However, I know of few parents who could so decide. The vast majority of American parents today are not spiritually prepared to make such a decision. Most would have saved Ike's life but not his leg—or his dreams. His life would have headed in a different direction, and America would have lost one of its greatest military commanders and the thirty-fourth president of the United States.

Over the years I have related this situation to a number of parents and asked how they would react. Virtually all of them said they would reluctantly tell the doctors to amputate.

Although most parents have not prepared their teenagers to accept responsibility for their lives and to recognize a deeper reality, clearly the Eisenhowers had. Even though Ike said he refused the amputation so he could play ball, my understanding of unique potential says that even at fifteen, his deeper vision of his future told him he needed that leg.

It is no coincidence that both Blanche's parents and Dwight Eisenhower's lived on a farm. This farm upbringing no doubt instilled in them a deep humility and respect for a power and a purpose beyond themselves. Perhaps because farmers recognize that their livelihood is totally dependent upon nature, over which they have no control, they more easily accept that neither can they control the growth of their children. Just as nature rules the farm, destiny dictates the proper development of a child's uniqueness, which parents alter at their peril.

Learning to Let Go

Learning to let go, to resist controlling our children, is an essential step in becoming a spiritual parent. But to take this step we must first let go of our own parents and childhood.

The primary function of the family is to help children fulfill their unique potential. But when parents still harbor adolescent attitudes, they tend to allow other priorities—careers, outside interests, or the marriage itself—to infringe on this primary function. When this happens, serious problems will be created for all family members. A child cannot raise a child; the parent's unresolved adolescent issues will inevitably cause the child to follow in the parent's footsteps, thus diverting the natural development of the child's destiny.

Consider this cycle: The husband and wife have marital problems, rooted in the unresolved issues of their own upbringing. Their children serve as a preoccupation and a relief from these problems. They may even induce the children (albeit unwittingly) to create additional problems in order to

distract the parents from their own. When it comes time to let go of their children, one or both parents will unconsciously resist, because this means returning to the marriage problems. The children may unconsciously feel that by leaving home, they are betraying their parents. Thus they carry guilt into their new marriages and repeat the cycle with their own children.

Here is another scenario: Mom supports Dad's view that his career is being held back by an unappreciative boss (when in fact it is due to his own deficiencies). In return, Dad never questions whether Mom is really challenging herself. This pattern of protection ultimately affects the entire family. Because neither mate is striving to "be the best I can be," the lives of both feel incomplete. The parents then turn to their children to provide the love and sense of accomplishment they themselves are missing. The children naturally respond and attempt to become what their parents want them to be. But this ultimately leaves the children unfulfilled, and their growing frustration will seek expression through whatever outlet is available, such as sex, drugs, or crime.

So adult control ends up compromising the unique potential of each family member and limits children to becoming weaker versions of their parents rather than seeking their own unique destinies. Such entanglements exist in all families to some degree. Unless they are confronted and dealt with, they will contaminate the next family generation.

Easier Said Than Done

Resolving control issues is easier said than done. The process of letting go can be intensely difficult. It means turning your back on what you've learned or accomplished and embarking on uncharted and often frightening new waters. It's like choosing between a comfortable old chair and a new perch appearing neither familiar nor secure.

Letting go of one stage of life and moving on to the next can be painful. Families naturally resist change, which is why we have rituals such as christenings, weddings, and funerals to help us let go of one stage of life and enter another.

It is difficult even for well-adjusted teenagers to let go

of their protective dreamworld and face the harsh realities of adult life. Likewise, it is tough for the healthiest of parents to let go of their adolescent children and face the necessity of reexamining the purpose of their own lives. In some cases, parents continue searching for excuses to "help" their kids, long after the children should begin leading independent lives. The fact that so many young adults still live at home highlights the spiritual failure often found in American parenting.

In counseling families, I find latent immaturity even in the most dedicated parents, which adversely affects their kids. The real problem isn't the parents' commitment, but rather their own inadequate preparation for adulthood.

In the movie *Roots,* the young Kunta Kinte and his peers are taken into the jungle by tribal elders. When Kunta returns he scorns his mother's embrace, which he sees as an insult to his newfound status as an emerging warrior. This African ritual helps the boy to become a man.

Although Americans have rituals to accompany birth, marriage, and death, for most of us there is no rite of passage from adolescence into adulthood. I suspect the ancient Jewish custom of bar mitzvah was established to help parents begin the process of letting go and to jar the youngster into the reality of personal accountability. But for most Americans outside the Jewish faith, the only standard for passing into adulthood is to meet arbitrary academic requirements.

In the thousands of families I have counseled, I have found very few parents who have effectively let go and grown beyond their own parents even after their parents have passed away. I found it very difficult to let go of my family's unrealistic expectations; moreover, my parents were alcoholics. I believe that both of these factors contributed to my being a late bloomer.

Ask yourself if you are capable of evaluating your own parents in terms of their upbringing, principles, and dreams. If you still see them more as personalities related to you, rather than as separate individuals, you probably haven't yet let go and grown beyond your own family entanglements—the primary prerequisite for becoming a spiritual parent.

Ego versus Principle

As parents learn to let go and give up their need for control, they begin to allow their principles and convictions, rather than their egos, to guide their parenting. It is amazing how even little children can instinctively tell the difference.

One morning when Malcolm was about three, I was late for class. He had crawled into bed with Blanche and was watching me frantically trying to get dressed. I couldn't find what I wanted and was becoming more frustrated by the minute. When I opened the drawer that was filled with my socks, none of which matched, I finally exploded. I started angrily throwing them on the floor: "I wish [throw] I had [throw] two socks [throw] that matched!" Whereupon Malcolm said to me, "If you act that way about it, you won't get any!" Blanche threw the sheet up over her head, and I stood there like a chastened child.

This story illustrates that Malcolm was not only aware of his father's ego but understood that it is okay to challenge it. Rarely can a child in the typical American family get away with chastising an angry parent! In the typical, ego-oriented family, parents rather than principles are the ultimate authorities children must obey. But Malcolm knew, even at this early age, that our family operated on principle rather than personality or ego, and that Blanche and I would have to follow the same guidelines we set for him. This helped him let go of his parents and accept responsibility for his own life when he became a young adult.

Such deeper lessons—just like entanglements—are passed from generation to generation. When my grandson Zach was about the same age, my daughter Laurie was stranded on the highway with a flat tire. Her husband couldn't figure out how to use the new jack. After observing this for some ten minutes, Zach remarked, "Mom, we're in trouble. Dad doesn't know what he's doing!"

When parents raise their children according to principles, they are consistent in their discipline, because their judgment is based on the same steady principles. By contrast, parents who rely on their egos in raising children are inconsistent.

Their discipline may vary dramatically, depending on their mood or on other, external concerns, such as work-related problems or a preoccupation over what the neighbors think. Such inconsistency is confusing to the children, who never know what to expect from Mom and Dad and who are never given any guiding principles to internalize.

Although consistency in parenting is important, it must be blended with a deep sense of humility. Parents must acknowledge that they might make the wrong decisions while trying to adhere to their principles. In addition, they must respect their children's independent spirits.

Blanche and I believed in firm and consistent family discipline—Blanche could sometimes quell unruly behavior with a sharp glance—but our children also knew we enjoyed their expressions of imagination and independence, like Malcolm's running account of his imaginary friend, George the Fox, until the sad day when he announced, "George has gone away, and he's never coming back"; Laurie's once having the entire school searching the campus for her, until we finally found her hiding behind a curtain in her room (she probably wasn't getting enough attention); and ten-year-old Gigi's determined march into the local auto dealership to see the Corvette she was planning to buy someday. While guiding our children to adopt our values, we also encouraged them to develop a world beyond their parents.

Becoming an Adult

Children's independence must be encouraged from a very early age, but until they become adolescents they are incapable of assuming true responsibility for their own growth. They are primarily reactors rather than actors.

My experience has taught me that by about age thirteen, most youngsters begin to develop the capability of thinking and acting for themselves. For the next six years or so, parents should gradually transfer accountability so that the children learn to become self-governing individuals. By the age of nineteen or twenty, the children should be assuming at least 51 percent of the responsibility for their own lives. If they are not accepting the majority responsibility by that age, it may take a life crisis to accomplish the transfer—if it ever occurs.

Although parents should gradually increase their adolescent's responsibility and accountability during this period, the child should recognize the parent as the majority stockholder. An example will convey what I mean.

There was a time in our marriage when Blanche was struggling with alcoholism and we were separated. My teenage daughter Gigi was living with me. Without the foundation Blanche had afforded our family, Gigi and I struggled with our new relationship. Even though Gigi was respecting the letter of my authority, it seemed that she was only selectively listening to my guidance. I finally confronted her:

"Gigi, make a decision. If you really think you know best for yourself, then ignore my advice and trust yourself, but accept the consequences. You will make mistakes, but if you take responsibility, they will be the right ones.

"But if you don't think you know best how to make decisions at this point, recognize you can't yet trust yourself and find someone whose guidance you *can* trust. Obviously, I think that should be me. But whatever you do, do us both a service and stop calling the shots while listening to me only when you have to."

Gigi decided she was not yet ready to accept responsibility for her life. She began truly to hear my advice, even if she didn't always agree with it or accept it, and our relationship changed for the better.

Several years later, when she was in college, Gigi wanted

to switch her major from liberal arts to merchandising. We had several long discussions over my concerns, including my belief that liberal arts is a foundation for finding oneself and that specialization should come later.

She finally said, "Dad, I really feel the change is right for me; I'm just not motivated to do liberal arts." I backed off, knowing she had listened to me, and I sensed that she was listening to her conscience. It makes no difference that she later came to believe I was right and she was wrong; she had accepted the full consequences of her decision and the responsibility for her life.

The Bond of Family Trust

Gigi trusted in my guidance during those formative years. Likewise, I trusted her to make her own decisions if she felt she was ready, while letting her know I was there to help if she felt she was not. Such a bond of mutual trust helps both parents and children to weather the demanding trials of adolescence.

When Malcolm was in his late teens, he once asked me if he could use the car when Blanche was away. I hesitated, which the kids knew would probably lead to a yes answer, because I was the easy one. Malcolm saw my hesitation and added, "Well, I asked Mom for the car a week ago [explaining the circumstances] and she said no." Whereupon I said, "Oh, then no." Malcolm continued, "Dad, I don't agree." He then proceeded to say why. I nodded, and the conversation was over. But he knew I would discuss with Blanche whether he should be given more elbow room.

Malcolm would have violated our trust by not telling me about his mother's "no," even though he knew it would probably kill his plans. He knew I wanted to say yes, but helping him grow up properly was not just my job; he had to help me with it. Surely our own family doesn't always operate at this high level, nor must it necessarily. But there has to be a bond of real trust if the child is to make a smooth transition to becoming an adult.

Unfortunately, the erosion of this deeper trust in American families today is such that most youngsters wouldn't resist manipulating the situation to get the car. In high schools I visit, I find roughly 90 percent of American young people would not take a serious personal problem to a parent—and further admit their parents are unaware of how they, the students, are really conducting their social lives. This atmosphere makes the question of adult manipulation by youngsters only a matter of degree.

I am compelled to add here how incredibly blind today's society is to this deeper erosion of trust. Young people have generally given up trying to explain it to adults, and a powerful youth culture has filled this gap and taken control. The increasingly unsafe school environments for students signal the tragic consequences.

The Power of Example

Children learn to trust their parents by perceiving that the parents are trustworthy, that is, that their actions reflect the principles and beliefs they espouse. Children learn by example. When there is a conflict between words and actions, kids will instinctively follow what the parents practice, not what they preach.

A Model of Dishonesty

Perhaps my most memorable experience of how children learn by example (in this case a *bad* example) occurred when my son Malcolm was nine years old. One day I noticed that Malcolm's friend Phil was wearing my old watch, and I asked him where he got it. Phil replied, "Malcolm gave it to me."

I found my son and asked testily, "Malcolm, did you give Phil my old watch?" preparing to give him a lecture on ownership. But Mal quietly said, "No, I didn't, Dad."

When I confronted Phil, he burst into tears but stuck to his version of the story, so I took the problem to his father. Mr. P., angrily eyeing his son (who was often in trouble), began offering profuse apologies to me. Feeling magnanimous, I said we ought to ask an impartial person, the boys' principal, to determine the truth.

Mr. P. and I waited half an hour before the principal came

out of his office to tell us he had almost extracted a confession from Phil. But a short while later the principal, looking relieved, emerged again, followed by a bawling Malcolm and a quieter Phil and announced, "Malcolm admitted giving Phil the watch."

I had never been so thunderstruck by anything in my entire life. Blanche and I raised our children to tell the truth above all else; they knew a lie was the only spanking offense.

My first passing thought was that God had given me a lemon (which showed where my ego was). The principal tried to reassure me in my distraught state: "If Mal were fourteen or fifteen, I'd be concerned, but this situation is quite common at his age." I appreciated his sensitivity, but I rejected the message. If Blanche and I took such pride in our parenting, how could we not share the responsibility for our children's failures?

We spent a day with Malcolm, trying to understand what had happened. This much was clear: Malcolm chose to lie to his father over a minor incident rather than trust the truth. Superficially, it seemed that his father's approval was more important to Malcolm than his respect for the truth. But at a deeper level I knew that I must have been setting some example of lying.

When you think that you are honest and that you revere the truth, it is not easy to locate your own lies. But once I accepted that I was the model for Malcolm's dishonesty, I quickly uncovered my own. I would often say, "Malcolm, I don't care what you do or how well you do it, as long as it's your best." It sounded good; it's what a parent ought to believe. But in my case, it was a lie.

If Malcolm were to come home with all *D*'s on his report card and the teacher said it was his best, I know that secretly I would have been disappointed. If someday he failed to get into a top-notch college, it would make a difference to me, whether I admitted it or not. I thought about the time Malcolm came up to bat in a Little League All Star game and looked at me before he even looked at the pitcher. Was he really learning from me that doing your best was more important than doing well?

I didn't feel very good about myself at this point. But I

confronted my ego and resolved to resist making my son's accomplishments part of my trophy collection and to help him respect the very best in himself, wherever it took him and whatever the consequences.

Malcolm lied again, later, but this time I shared the responsibility; as I continued to root out my own subtle forms of dishonesty, Malcolm quickly rid himself of the habit. I am pleased to say that today I think the quality most admired in all three of our children is their honesty and integrity.

Victory over Fear

To serve as a model for our children's character development, we must consistently work on our own development. My years of teaching experience had taught me that the growth of students parallels the growth of their teachers, at school *and* at home. But the lesson really sank in when Malcolm was fourteen.

I had decided to face my fear of heights by climbing an eighty-foot cliff at Hurricane Island in Maine. My fear of heights had begun to make me doubt my own courage, and I believed those doubts would eventually hold back my children and my students, just as my dishonesty had served as a model for Malcolm's lying. That's why I chose that eighty-foot cliff to confront my fears—it scared me more than anything else in the world.

At the time, Malcolm lacked self-confidence, so part of my plan was to take him along with me to let him see me at my worst, thus cutting me down to a size he could more readily identify with. I also thought that having him there would reinforce my own commitment to follow through.

Increasingly the climb exposed my fear, exhausting me emotionally as well as physically. At the most dangerous point, I was hanging out over a ledge and found myself unable to make the somewhat complicated moves to follow my son across the precipice. Because failure here would probably mean death, my moment of truth had come.

My eyes pleaded wildly with my Outward Bound guide to give me an excuse to get off the cliff, but to no avail; he knew why I was there. Panic- stricken, I considered faking an injury, but quickly realized I couldn't leave my son with lifelong doubts about his father.

I then thought of simply telling Malcolm I didn't have the guts to make the moves. But this placed my fears and concern over my personal safety above my deeper convictions. I recalled the biblical warning that "the sins of the fathers will be visited on the sons." How could I live with myself, knowing that my failure of courage today would one day inhibit the growth of my child?

I sickened when I realized the only option left was to try that ridge. But was my problem really fear? Maybe it was a lack of physical ability. What if I killed myself? With my responsibilities, did I have the right to gamble my life? In a cold sweat and panicky voice, I told my guide, "Look, I'm not one of your kids. I'm forty-one years old and my muscles are dead tired. Are you sure I can make those moves? Are you sure it's my fear that's the problem?"

Unfortunately, he was sure. I realized the guide knew my fear was making my own judgment unsound. I also recognized that he wouldn't take the risk of encouraging me if he felt I were incapable of making the physical moves, since the result would be certain death. These thoughts reassured me, enabling me to trust the guide and succeed in honoring my commitment to myself and my son. (Fortunately, I found out only later they normally require safety ropes for this maneuver, or I wouldn't have done it.)

What began as a terrifying experience turned out to be a richly rewarding one, for me and for Malcolm. I think I taught him there are no supermen, just ordinary men trying to do extraordinary things. Our relationship improved, his confidence grew, and his life took a much better turn.

As for me, I still fear heights, but I no longer fear fear itself, thanks to my commitment to spiritual parenting. If Malcolm hadn't been present that day, I wouldn't have made the climb—and I wouldn't have gained the deeper self-confidence that comes from facing and conquering our fears.

This experience also made me realize how deeply I cared for my children. When they were little, I remember looking at them once and wondering, Do I actually love them? I had the horrible feeling that in a life-or-death situation, I might try

Malcolm and Joe Gauld today.

to save myself first. But the cliff experience confirmed for me that spiritual parents develop an automatic reflex to protect their children, like instinctively raising an arm to ward off a bullet, sacrificing the hand to save the head. On that eighty-foot cliff, I finally came to know at a deep level that I would rather risk my life than leave Malcolm with the wrong example for his life.

Spirituality and the American Parent

Spiritual parenting requires that we serve as role models for our children, setting the example we wish them to follow. Preparing children for the experience of being adult Americans further requires that we inspire their spiritual belief in the proposition that "all men are created equal." How do we do this? By demonstrating, through our actions, that we share this belief in equality.

My crisis of conscience in 1962 led me to give up an assured career to find a better way of schooling for American kids. Malcolm faced a similar crisis after college, when he gave up a promising teaching job to face his fear of joining the Hyde crusade. Later I learned that my handling of the earlier crisis gave him the strength to handle his. Malcolm explains:

> I can well remember when my father was just a regular teacher in a regular school. What stands out most clearly was his deep desire to be a headmaster, inquiring about schools as far away as the West Coast.
>
> I didn't then perceive my father as having any unique ideas for bettering American education. In fact, I envisioned him as maintaining the traditional form, setting up shop with us as "the first family" on some campus.
>
> When I was around ten, it looked as though my father would land a headmastership in Florida. Pops was so excited over the prospect he could barely control himself. I tried to fake enthusiasm; after all, I was proud he was going to be a headmaster. But I shuddered at the very idea of leaving rural New England.
>
> Then, right after returning from Florida, Mom and Dad had one of their "serious" conversations in the living room. Their expressions told me that we wouldn't be moving, at least to Florida. I heard them use some big-sounding words. The word that stood out was *segregated*—the reason Dad had refused the job.
>
> I was so proud of my father for refusing to work at a school that wouldn't admit blacks, I bragged about it to all my friends. I didn't know if they understood my enthusiasm, but I didn't really care.
>
> Perhaps my father believed all of this slipped over my head or perhaps he didn't view it as a major decision on his part. But I needed that example. I had liked being the son of the head coach, teacher, administrator, but that image had a hollow ring. It was

> his losing the Florida job that gave me something I
> could really understand, look up to, and follow.

Incredibly, Malcolm was perceiving a change in me I was not then aware of myself. Segregation was yet to become a big issue; had my career come first, my ego might have rationalized that I could take the job and then integrate the school. But my deeper instincts knew that such a compromise would jeopardize the entire concept of unique potential. I didn't understand all of this at the time, but Malcolm, at age ten, did! My actions were the basis for his later decision.

Separating Opinion from Principle

In the process of instilling American values in our children, we must carefully separate our own personal expressions of patriotism from our deeper principles and give children the elbow room to develop an integrity of their own. My wife recalled:

> I was a hawk during the early part of the Vietnam
> War. I trusted my government, but more than that, I
> remembered three well-loved men who had gone to war
> in the 1940s, never to return. Dad and my two older
> brothers died trying to erase the belief in racial
> supremacy.
> Our son Malcolm began testing my feelings about
> the Vietnam War when he saw the draft as part of his
> future. I said, "If you run to Canada with your tail
> between your legs, I'll disown you. You will be my son
> only in a biological sense."
> Joe helped me to be a bit more logical. I would
> accept Malcolm's decision to be a conscientious
> objector. If he morally rejected the war, stayed in the
> United States, and chose prison, I would admire his
> strength of character and be there every visiting day.
> But if I ignored my personal convictions and
> supported his decision to run to Canada, I could no
> longer look to Gettysburg with honest pride. Instead, I
> would face the crosses with lowered eyes and with a

profound sense of national shame. If he chose Canada, I would have to disown him.

To disown my only son would be an excruciatingly painful act from which I might not recover. But the decision would come from the depth of my inner being, over which I have no control, from something far greater than my strong desire for the safety and security of those I adore.

This last sentence is the powerful statement of a spiritual parent. Blanche was acknowledging her conscience as the voice of a higher power, one she had to obey even above her motherly instincts. Like Abraham, Blanche was truly accepting the role of assistant in raising her children.

As spiritual parents we have strong beliefs, but we must also recognize our own limitations and be ready and willing to revise our beliefs. Having lost two brothers and a father in World War II, Blanche naturally had strong feelings about the Vietnam War. But I helped her to see that Malcolm had to express his own independent conscience.

Malcolm wasn't then old enough to be seriously considering his options over Vietnam. What was really going on was a family learning to separate opinions from principles in the process of letting go.

We Are Not Alone

Two things are certain if we strive to be spiritual parents and help our children achieve their best: we will run into problems, and we'll need help in solving them.

To accomplish great things requires exceptional vision and boldness. With these come exceptional problems, as demonstrated by the lives of historical giants like Winston Churchill (who failed a grade twice), Albert Einstein (who flunked algebra), Thomas Edison (who was a school dropout), and Eleanor Roosevelt (who had an unhappy childhood).

The more a family attempts to achieve, the more struggles and challenges parents will face and the more the family will need to draw on outside resources for support. As an old proverb reminds us, It takes a whole village to raise a child.

Unfortunately, in America our image of a good family is one that doesn't have problems. Nor does it seek outside help, for to do so would be an admission of defeat. Like Rambo, the family triumphs singlehandedly.

This prevailing image of the "good" family is tragically stunting America's growth. Because of this distorted image, families often have to become disaster areas before they acknowledge their problems and seek help in solving them.

Parents need the humility to recognize when they need to go outside themselves for assistance. I speak from experience. Blanche's and my failure to accept such powers beyond ourselves nearly destroyed our family.

Early in our marriage, Blanche was a very controlled drinker, while I tended to abuse alcohol. I failed to notice that her drinking was gradually passing mine and getting out of control, until she was nearly the alcoholic my mother was. Then, in our ignorance, we both threw gasoline on the fire: we tried to beat her disease by sheer willpower, with my "help" making her problem worse, until our family was sucked into a whirlpool of problems.

We finally "surrendered" and our faith led us to the help we needed, in the form of Alcoholics Anonymous and Al-Anon. Fortunately, we were a Hyde family at the time, so the school community also helped our children free their own spirit and conscience from the family maelstrom.

Our family struggle with alcoholism made us all better people. Looking back now, it is hard to believe that two dedicated and concerned parents like Blanche and me could subject ourselves and our children to such craziness over a ten-year span. In typical American fashion we let our pride fool us into believing that somehow we could solve our own problems, thus denying the wealth of help and understanding of so many others around us.

We human beings weren't meant to be perfect. Many of our family problems today are the result of family dynamics that we experienced in childhood and over which we had no control. We should never tie our pride to our problems and shortcomings but only to how we deal with them.

My mother was a compassionate woman with a wonderful sense of humor and a deep understanding of people. Her love of life and her independent spirit were an inspiration to all of her children.

But there was another side to her, a dark side: she was an alcoholic and a binge drinker. I believed I had two mothers: the fun-loving, vivacious, and compassionate one, and the weepy, out-of-control impersonator whom I could barely recognize. I would pray on my way home from school that my real mother would be there.

Now and then, Mother might suffer a blackout and end up miles from home. Once, after she had been missing for three days, I heard a noise in the basement and went downstairs to find her trying to sneak into her own house. She saw me and burst into uncontrollable tears. At that moment I realized the depth of her unhappiness and understood that alcohol must be beyond her control. From then on I didn't take her drinking so personally, and some of my resentment of her changed to pity.

Growing up, I was mortified by the public scenes of Mother's alcoholism, and how the neighbors must have gossiped about "those crazy Gaulds." But even though my childhood was tough, today I appreciate the humanizing process brought about by our family problems—it's like preferring old, beat-up Raggedy Ann to the shiny new doll.

My growing up taught me never to judge individuals by their mistakes or problems but rather by how they deal with them. For this reason, Hyde School is committed to helping parents and children deal with any and every aspect of their lives.

CHAPTER 7

Hyde Parents Meet the Challenge

Hyde has shown me that letting go doesn't mean not caring. It means caring enough to give my child the freedom to fail or to fly.

—A Hyde parent

If I were going to ask my son to accept challenges, take risks, open up, and share, I found I had to ask it of myself too.

—A Hyde parent

He stood frozen—that is, aside from the involuntary twitch in his left leg that caused his knee to vibrate back and forth like an eggbeater. He was a victim of sensory overload, and emotions raced through his consciousness—fear, excitement, apprehension, embarrassment, desire, humiliation.

His anger at himself for his own inability to act was becoming his dominant feeling. The task was so simple! He had only to let go of one hanging rope for a split second, quickly inch his way about eighteen inches to his left and then grasp another rope identical to the one he was currently using as a tether. The fact that he was simultaneously standing on a tightrope thirty-five feet above the ground was the primary source of his temporary inability to perform this task.

"Go for it! I've got you . . ." came a voice from below. The belay line, a safety rope connecting the man on the tightrope with the owner of the voice by means of a pulley secured above the monkey vine, offered some comfort, but still the twitch was the only discernable movement from above. He thought to himself, It didn't look this high off the ground before I climbed the ladder!

The voice from below continued. "Go ahead, Dad. You can do it!" That did it. An inner force took over. Placing his life in his son's hands in a most literal sense, the man let go of the rope he was clutching and reached for the vine.

This vignette was written by my son, Malcolm, about a Hyde father who had just gone through our ropes course, part of Hyde's intensive parent involvement program. The course is designed to establish a bond of trust between parent and child by making the child responsible for the life of the parent and the parent dependent upon the child for his or her safety.

The anecdote stops short of telling what happened to Dad, because it doesn't matter. Sometimes Dad (or Mom) grabs the second vine triumphantly and goes on to conclude the ropes course with a thrilling pulley ride down the "zip line." Other times he stumbles and is caught by the belay line held by his child. And occasionally he simply can't go through with the exercise at all and climbs down the ladder with hopes of giving it another try in the future. No matter what the outcome, the son or daughter will likely be inspired by the parent's effort. By exhibiting courage and risking vulnerability, the parent has served as a powerful role model for the child.

Leading by example is the root of all successful parenting. But today's wide gulf between the generations and their conflicting values speak to our national ignorance of this simple truth. Good parents rightly expect much from their kids; but unless they expect the same things from themselves, a deep and possibly even unconscious parent-child conflict will develop. Parents end up blaming the attitude and behavior of youngsters; youngsters shift the blame back to parents who "don't understand" them. Each keeps expecting the other to change, and the child's growth becomes stagnant in this never-ending argument. But once parents begin to focus on their own growth, this argument suddenly disappears. Kids soon realize it's time to get moving, and now they have the example of parents to follow.

The Family Learning Program

After a decade of experience with kids like Matt, Len, and Bart (highlighted in Chapter 5), we clearly realized that Hyde could not foster the character development of students without also addressing the character of their parents. For this reason, today Hyde School accepts only families, not just students (at Hyde, we define "family" as one growing child and one committed adult). Once admitted to the school, Hyde parents must participate in an intensive, ongoing family learning program, consisting of family weekends, visits to Hyde's Family Learning Center, participation in regional groups of Hyde parents, annual parent retreats, and a program of self-reflection.

Family Weekends

Twice a year—once in the fall and once in the spring—every Hyde family comes to the campus in Bath, Maine, for a four-day weekend consisting of family seminars, performing arts activities, athletic competitions, and community meetings.

The weekend provides an opportunity for parents to visit Hyde, see what their children are like within the school community, get to know their teachers, and receive evaluations of their children's progress. Likewise, teachers have a chance to get to know the parents better; this personal knowledge of each student's family is essential for the teacher's role in guiding students toward the fulfillment of their unique potential. But the focal points of the weekends are family seminars in which parents and students together explore a broad range of family issues.

Buried Resentment   These meetings sometimes unearth painful conflicts that have been buried for years. Once a troubling issue is exposed to the light of day, it can be effectively addressed and resolved. A father writes:

> In one family seminar, a student, prodded by a teacher, finally opened up. In tears, he released his anger and frustration at his father's death and his resentment for his father's having left him and his mother. I then reflected on my own downhill relationship with my father, and it dawned on me I resented him the same way.
>
> My mother died when I was thirteen, and for three months my brother and I were left to fend for ourselves as our father grieved. It soon became obvious we needed a more stable life; eventually, an aunt raised both of us along with her own five children.
>
> I kept thinking about this after the seminar and took a trip to discuss it with my brother. I was amazed to learn he felt as I did: we both feel our father, in his anguish, "forgot" about us and just dropped out of living.

> Although the hurt is still there, I came to understand my father's feelings when I went through a similar disorienting period after my divorce, and I have forgiven him.

The unresolved childhood resentment of this man over his father's negligence had led him to be overly protective of his own children's feelings, thus denying them the opportunity to become emotionally independent. Parents who were abandoned in this way will often try to overcompensate for their earlier loss by smothering their kids. As a result, they end up re-creating in the kids the very feelings of insecurity they were trying to prevent by "protecting" them.

A Person, Not Just a Parent   The family seminars also give parents the opportunity to explore their own unique potential, which in some cases has been suppressed in the process of raising their children. A mother writes:

> My first parent-student seminar was an eye-opener. When a parent asked me to describe myself, I amazingly could not. With a sigh, I said it seemed I had been a parent my whole life; I had so tied my identity to my children that their failures and achievements had become my own.
> Sharing my discovery with a roomful of people was not only meaningful, but they seemed to offer a way in which I could help myself, while allowing my children to help themselves. In that seminar my own daughter told me to learn to be "selfish."
> It was like getting permission to be my own person! What a relief to unload the burden of feeling responsible for my children's behavior, and to give *them* the responsibility. I want my children to think for themselves, but it has more meaning when I give them the responsibility along with the independent thinking involved.

"I Thought I Was the Only One with Problems"   It's not uncommon for parents to feel a deep sense of relief once they've begun to share their struggles with other families. Learning

they aren't the only ones with problems is often the most important step in accepting themselves and resolving their problems. A mother writes:

> For me, the most helpful part of Hyde has been all the sharing in groups over the years. I went to Hyde thinking everyone else was all put together and I was the only one with problems. I felt like a failure as a mother and as a person.
>
> After listening to many people over the past four years share their feelings of failure, inadequacy, fears, and hurts, I feel I'm not so bad after all.
>
> My perfectionist tendencies had led me to have unrealistic expectations of myself and my family; we were defeated before we started. I have learned from Hyde that it is all right to be human and that failure is a better teacher than success. The strange thing about accepting failure in my life is that I feel far more successful. My children are doing well and my husband and I have grown.

The Family Learning Center

In addition to attending family weekends, Hyde parents gather at our on-campus Family Learning Center (FLC) for one three-day session during the school year. During their time here, they participate in seminars, physical activities, and writing projects, and continue to work with other parents and students and with their own children on personal and family issues.

As pointed out in previous chapters, our experience has shown that the attitudes and problems of students reflect those of their parents, which are in turn rooted in the dynamics of the parents' families of origin. Therefore, at FLC sessions, we ask parents to examine their own childhood issues and their relationships with their parents, so they can see the connection between their upbringing and their parenting. There's a saying often repeated at Hyde: The apple doesn't fall far from the tree.

Over the years the Family Learning Center has taught us

the profound interrelatedness of the family; whatever affects one member affects all. This influence can span generations; the real root of a kid acting out in school could be the unresolved issue of a great-grandparent!

With a bit of work, we're all capable of recognizing and correcting the character flaws and negative attitudes we've carried into adulthood. However, it's more difficult to identify the effects of negative or traumatic childhood experiences that we still carry in our subconscious minds. These childhood scars, if left undiscovered and unattended, can have negative effects on our children, as the following stories illustrate:

The Imaginary Burden   The B.s were a successful and highly respected suburban family, but they came to Hyde in total confusion. Their son, after years of academic and athletic success, seemed to go completely off track in ninth grade. He began running with questionable friends and had flunked his academic courses that year.

In a soul-searching interview, I helped the B.s to realize their son had a drug problem. After convincing them to place the son in an intensive drug rehabilitation program and for them to attend Al-Anon, I accepted the family for the fall term.

The B.s' deeper family issues surfaced at the Family Learning Center. In one seminar dealing with vision, Mr. B. walked to the blackboard and wrote "1991." This turned out to be the year when his plan for financial security for his family would finally be accomplished. Upon being questioned, Mr. B. acknowledged that 1991 would mark his fiftieth birthday, the age when his own father suddenly died. When pressed further, he insisted he felt no sense of abandonment or bitterness over his father's death.

The next day, Mr. B. told of a sudden urge he had experienced while driving in the country, to chuck his job as an advertising executive and become a bush pilot (he had been a pilot in the military). I asked if he saw any connection between this urge and his son's problems with drugs. He said he didn't.

In time, Mr. B. began to see that his resentment over his father's death had left him with the imagined burden of insuring his own children wouldn't face a similar hardship. This burden depressed his spirit and affected his son's. Unconsciously oppressed by the father's burden, the son instinctively rejected the "responsible" path in school and, following his father's bush pilot spirit, drifted into the glamorous world of drugs.

The father finally realized that to help his son, he needed to address and let go of his own childhood. The more he and his wife worked on their own growth, the more responsible the son became at Hyde and the less he was involved with drugs; eventually he gave them up completely.

"Sometimes I Just Wanted You to Say No . . ." For many Hyde students, the FLC sessions provide the first opportunity they've ever had to speak openly and honestly to their parents. Such honesty, although painful at times, ultimately has a profound effect on healing the family's wounds. A father writes:

At our first three-day FLC weekend, we were in our family counseling group session. My wife, our son, and I were all seated in a circle with the other ten or so families. It was our turn to talk about each of our perceptions of family issues.

I jumped in to go first, as usual. I began pontificating about progress, and our son interrupted: "Oh bullshit, Dad. You always talk and sound good and look good, and my friends think you're okay, but I don't even know what you stand for. I can tell what you've accomplished, but what are your values, what are your principles?

"Leadership? You never show leadership . . . you always duck the issues and hide in your rowing or reading. Courage? Sure, you flew jets off carriers, but you're afraid to confront me, like when my brother and I fight. Dad! Listen! Sometimes I just wanted you to say no to me."

At this point I broke down and sobbed, the first time I—the fighter pilot—had done that in front of a group. And my wife started to cry, and so did my son—and then everybody else too. I hugged my son and thanked him, and couldn't stop crying for a while.

The truth hurt, but after that I did feel a load off my shoulders and became more aware of my behavior. I began to take leadership in the family and showed more willingness to initiate family confrontations. Without the opportunity for my son to open up and share his feelings courageously in the FLC forum, I would never have made this breakthrough, which I consider one of the most important moments of my life.

The Closest of Friends In many cases, parents and students forge deep bonds once they learn how to open up as a result of participating in the Family Learning Center. A student writes:

One night, after my mother returned from a long day of soul-searching at an FLC session, I confronted her with the fact that neither of us had cried over my father's death and that I had barely known who he was. We both broke down and cried and had one of the best soul-to-soul conversations and reconnections we had ever had. I learned more in those few hours than I had ever known about the excellent person that my father had been. My mother and I had an intense bond that had been shut off for many years by pain and denial. It was then liberated in the joy and the excitement of starting a relationship anew. We became the closest of friends after that and truly got down to feeling so much of what we had blocked out for so long.

Regional Groups

In order to continue their work on personal and family issues while away from the campus, all Hyde parents attend monthly meetings with other parents who live in their particular region of the country. These parent groups meet at least once a month to share their understanding and experience of the Hyde process, to challenge one other, and to work on their personal growth, through seminars, writing assignments, and physical activities. Many parents continue their growth work during lunches and dinners or through frequent telephone conversations.

Pooling Wisdom   By working as a team, each parent in the group can benefit from the experience of the others. Even a small suggestion from another parent can make a significant impact, as one mother explains:

I get the most out of taking part in my regional group. Our group members have taught me that by expressing true feelings and fears, I can learn many valuable lessons. Through some fathers' tears, I felt my own concerns surface. Through some mothers' laughter when they described their FLC sessions, I realized the struggle for happiness and better relationships was definitely worth it.

Sometimes in our group it's a small suggestion that

> goes a long way—for example, when one parent said, "If you want to get along better with your child, treat him as if he is somebody else's child." I decided to apply this to my own son over Christmas vacation. I found I was never more patient and understanding of him. I kept asking myself, If he were a friend's child would I listen to him better? Would I yell at him less? Would I trust him more? I realized the answer to all my questions was yes. It helped me to see my son in a different light.

"He's Trying to Control You!" The chair of each region is responsible for matching every new Hyde family with a veteran family, who will keep in touch with the newcomers and help them through the initial traumas of the Hyde process. This mentor program is important for two reasons. First, it raises the expectations of veteran parents; it asks that they more deeply internalize the Hyde process so they can serve as role models for other parents. It takes courage for veteran parents to share their family's issues and struggles with newcomers.

Second, veteran parents can serve as sounding boards for novice families, providing valuable advice and encouraging them to take the risk of opening up and exploring their own family issues. A Hyde mother writes of how a comment from her mentor enabled her for the first time to understand the dynamics of her relationship with her son:

> Manipulation and "peace at any price" have been a part of our family life ever since Gene was born—from early temper tantrums at age two until his teen years. He learned that by being difficult, he always got his way. But pacifying him all the time made family life unbearable.
>
> When Gene finished summer school at Hyde, he called and said, "Mom, I definitely am not going back." I hung up the phone with a sense of doom.
>
> When we came up to Hyde, the more we talked, the more adamant he became. Later, a parent who was guiding us through the process said, "He's trying to

control your lives." It was like a light flashed on, and I saw the truth.

At a seminar later, I broke down crying and told Gene, "You're manipulating us. We're like puppets, and you pull the strings." To my surprise, Gene started crying too and said, "Yes, that's true and I'm not very happy about it. I feel that you don't love me because you let me get away with it."

That one day reversed a twelve-year pattern and became a turning point in our relationship.

Parent Retreats

Once a year, usually in the winter months, each regional parent group meets for a three-day weekend at some neutral site, for several days of reflection and sharing. Initially the retreats were facilitated by Hyde teachers, but over time, parents began to take full responsibility for running them. Teachers still attend the retreats, but now they come as participants rather than leaders, as students rather than teachers.

Childhood Scars   The retreats, like other parts of the parent program at Hyde, often uncover powerful issues that have long been forgotten or ignored. A father writes:

At my Hyde retreat I attended a meeting at Joe Gauld's house and contributed nothing. Everyone present seemed to know I had a problem I had to face. I talked to Joe afterward and told him he just wouldn't understand. But instead of cutting me down, he said, "Just trust me and write a paper."

It was very hard to put into words a problem that had plagued me for twenty-five years. As a teenager I developed a chronic case of acne and became very self-conscious about it. I went from doctor to doctor for help, but all they really wanted was my money. The acne was a constant source of embarrassment and I felt people cut me deeply with their tongues.

As I matured the condition did clear, but I retained

the scars inside. I felt dirty and unclean. I couldn't look at people without feeling the lash of their tongues and the embarrassment.

At the seminar the next day I was asked to read my paper. I tried, but the only thing that came out of me was tears. After I partially gained control of myself, I read my paper with great pain. My son was present, so I just couldn't back down.

When I finished, it was a tremendous relief. Surprisingly, everyone in the group shared a similar situation they had experienced as teenagers.

It was a turning point in my life. I can now look at people and be in groups without feeling ashamed.

The father's account revealed the root of his son's problems. The father represented responsibility to the son. But by carrying around the imagined burden of his acne, he made the rewards of responsibility seem unattractive, thus unwittingly encouraging his son to remain irresponsible. Once he shed this burden, his life, and his son's, took a turn for the better.

Many parents mistakenly believe that what the child doesn't know won't hurt him. The truth is, we convey the *spirit* of our experiences to our children, whether or not we relate the actual experiences to them in words. By not communicating our experiences directly so our children can separate our problems from theirs, we are in effect passing our problems on to our kids, where they will reappear in disguised form, such as the irresponsibility of the son in the previous story. Because the kids don't know of the original problem, they have no way of solving their own, "disguised" problem, because the two are linked.

Self-Reflection

Self-reflection is an integral part of every aspect of the Hyde family learning program rather than a separate component of the program. I have often observed that providing students with new experiences gives them food for thought, material on which they can reflect and that serves as a catalyst for personal growth. The same is true for parents. The idea behind the family learning program is to provide parents with new experiences and challenges, then to have them reflect on what they've learned. All significant growth follows this cycle of action and reflection.

One vehicle for self-reflection is journaling. Hyde parents learn to make weekly journal entries dealing with personal growth topics, such as their personal goals, their hopes for their family life, and their expectations for their children.

Writing is an especially powerful tool for self-reflection and growth, as a Hyde parent points out:

> At the Family Learning Center, one of the counselors told me to start writing down my feelings as essays or letters to family members. He said, "Writing is different from thinking. On paper, more comes out."
>
> What a truth that is. I have written dozens of essays and letters since. When I read them, I am amazed at what I feel. As much as I disliked this process, I now realize it has become a vital part of me and will probably last forever.

Another parent confirms the power of the written word:

> The single most important part of the Hyde process for me is the written papers required for all Hyde meetings. I don't enjoy writing them, and I have to wrestle with the topics more often than not. But they do force me to be introspective and to consider my actions and inactions. And they make me honest with myself, which has been difficult for me. I don't always succeed, but if I do them the right way I'm able to get in touch with my feelings, vulnerabilities, and inadequacies.
>
> Revealing my true self to others always makes me feel very uncomfortable. The reactions and feedback of other people to what I write does help me focus on the truth of my observations and takes me to task on how I may be evading the truth. When I can consistently project the "real me" in these writing assignments, I'll know that the Hyde process is finally taking effect.

Honesty Is the Best (and Toughest) Policy

As Hyde parents became more experienced and more comfortable in sharing their lives with others in a group setting, they developed their own formal list of rules for participating in Hyde seminars. The guidelines were designed to ensure that every parent gets the maximum benefit from group encounters, by emphasizing honesty, responsibility, and openness:

Seminar Guidelines

1. When in doubt, I'll bet on the truth; still in doubt, I'll bet on more truth.
2. I'll share a part of myself and let others know how I feel about myself and them.
3. I will listen.
4. I will stay out of my ego as much as I can; I'll take my job, not myself, seriously.
5. I will not give advice, complain, explain, intellectualize, or protect.
6. I'll be specific and speak just for myself.
7. I'll stay on the subject.
8. I'll demand the best from others in the group. I'll focus on conscience, not emotion.
9. I have a personal obligation to make this seminar go.
10. I will try not to take things personally, respecting "If the shoe fits, wear it; if it doesn't, forget it."
11. I will maintain honest and open relationships with all seminar members.
12. I will respect confidentiality; what goes on here, stays here.

A Loving Confrontation

These rules can be tough to follow, and the emphasis on honesty sometimes leads to confrontations. But parents come to appreciate honest feedback, once they recognize it is offered in a spirit of love and concern rather than judgment. A Hyde mother writes of her feelings after being confronted by another parent in a seminar:

> Who does she think she is? How can she possibly know how I feel? Her husband didn't die; she never experienced antisemitism; she never feared rejection by an adopted child. How can she say I use those three excuses whenever I feel inadequate? She was using information I shared with her in private conversation.
>
> But that shakiness in her voice is not hostility, it is concern. I know she cares about me. She wouldn't risk our friendship if she didn't feel it was important to tell me this. I realized I had better get out of my ego and look at what was said.
>
> Well, I didn't see it overnight, or even in a week. But I finally understood what she was telling me: somewhere along the line I'd lost my zest for living and stopped looking forward to the future.

This mother's protection of herself had made her apathetic about her own life and contributed to her son's apathy. As she began to set a new, livelier example, her son started to confront his own complacency and to move from the motions stage to the effort stage at Hyde.

A Model of Defensiveness

Sometimes community meetings bring up volatile feelings, but even reluctant parents learn to overcome their defensiveness and face their problems with the help of the group. A father writes:

> At the meeting to discuss our attitudes and performance regarding parental admissions efforts, when my time came to talk, I quickly and accurately assessed my performance as poor. Another parent suggested that if I didn't do something to improve my attitude, maybe I should leave the group. I said little but got defensive and increasingly angry.
>
> After the meeting a student wanted to talk to me about my relationship with my son. I was impressed

with his integrity and amazed at his accuracy. I asked my son to join in.

We got into it and my son said to me, "You're angry." I responded, "You're God-damned right I am," rationalizing my position by questioning what gave the other parent the right to criticize me in the meeting. The more I talked, the more lethal I became.

By the time I retold this story to several other parents and my wife, I was really angry. But with their help, I began to see something. I thought of my son's defensiveness. I thought of his hiding behind anger. I thought of how he never put out more than a modest effort. I thought of how he has always run from the truth. I thought of his running from failure.

I finally decided: I think he needs a better model.

Stages of Parental Growth

Some parents who initially have the most negative response to group encounters end up getting the most out of them. A mother writes:

When first introduced to the Hyde process I thought it was touchy-feely BS. I had a strong negative reaction when people said "share" when they meant "tell," when they had "issues" instead of "problems." But I had no choice about participation if my son was to be able to stay at the school.

So I participated grudgingly and skeptically. At first, I faked the questions; instead of thinking deeply and writing something, I just made a few notes and then extemporized when it was my turn to speak. I did this so that I could have something to say that fit in with the flow of conversation. I never revealed anything personal that wasn't (in my opinion) complimentary. I thought the sessions were pretty tedious and didn't enjoy them, just put in the time. At least my relationship with my son began to improve.

Then it dawned on me that he was only a sophomore and that I was looking at three years of this stuff.

That's a lot of meetings for someone who was not inclined to this sort of thing. How was I going to survive? I decided the only way was to jump into it, to stop just dipping my toe in the water and dive headfirst into the icy pool.

So I started thinking seriously about my writing assignments. I did them in advance, and they were often several pages. When I finished a topic, I was sometimes miles away from where I had set off to be. I often junked the first few paragraphs when I saw how trivial they were. I often found myself very sad or even crying as I wrote.

At first I was scared to read this stuff publicly, but I found nothing but support. Nobody sneered or snickered. Nobody ran away in disgust. Nobody broke confidence. The comments I got were almost always helpful. Occasionally somebody would make a critical comment, and when I started to explain myself further or defend my position, the group wouldn't allow it.

It wasn't until later (sometimes weeks later) that I realized the critical comments were usually correct and very helpful. It was just that I hadn't been ready to hear them. I realized that the person who had the guts to tell me his or her feelings was the one who was giving me the most support. They weren't telling me what they thought I wanted to hear; they were telling me what they were really thinking and feeling.

I started giving my honest feedback to what others said. I found this very difficult when what I had to say was counter to what I thought they wanted to hear. But on several occasions I've been thanked later by people for giving them honest feedback. It feels good.

As I got more comfortable with the process, I found that I didn't think or worry about my son anymore. He was the reason I started this, but I had changed my focus; I was now doing it because I liked it. And the more I focused on myself and let him fend for himself, the better he got and the closer we became. Now I eagerly await Hyde meetings and find them incredibly refreshing and supportive.

In this story, we can see the mother growing from a parent who is simply going through the motions to one who is striving to get the most out of the Hyde program. Parents at Hyde, like teachers and students, go through distinct stages of understanding and commitment. Hyde parents have identified three basic stages of parental growth: self-evaluation, action, and leadership. These correspond to the three stages of growth of Hyde students that were discussed in Chapter 4 (motions, effort, and excellence).

Stage 1: Self-Evaluation

When they first arrive at Hyde, parents are expected to begin looking inward, to identify more clearly and deeply their behavioral, emotional, and spiritual strengths and weaknesses. During this self-evaluation stage, they are also expected to pursue humility, to recognize and share with others their strengths and limitations, their secret hopes and fears. One primary goal of this stage is to assist parents in differentiating the "real" aspects of themselves and their families from their public images, that is, the ones they show the neighbors.

Some specific requirements of stage 1: parents must share a written autobiography and complete journaling questions and occasional readings assigned by the FLC staff; they must take the Myers-Briggs Type Inventory, a personality test that helps them understand differences in individual temperament among family members; and they must participate in the required FLC sessions, family weekends, and regional meetings and retreats.

Each regional group also takes on a community service project in their local area, and each develops a ten-minute theatrical production that they perform during the Family Weekend in the spring. The entire school is inspired by the creativity and risk taking that Hyde parents display during these performances.

During this stage, new parents are matched with mentors. Mentors are veteran Hyde parents the newcomers have met in their regional groups or through the Family Learning Center.

Throughout stage 1, parents are expected to be active

participants in group meetings, sharing their own concerns and issues and soliciting the feedback of others. They may have a mild or strong aversion to doing so; all we ask is that they go through the motions.

Stage 2: Action

Stage 1 can be characterized as a time of inward reflection, increased awareness, and goal setting. Stage 2 is characterized by sharing outwardly, increased risk taking, and a strengthening of the parents' commitment to Hyde.

Completion of a personal written contract signals parents' entry into this action stage of growth. The personal contract outlines specific goals and changes the parents will seek during their tenure as Hyde parents.

During this stage, parents begin to take actions toward fulfilling the objectives of their personal contracts. While doing so, they continue their involvement in required FLC sessions, regional meetings, and retreats.

The amount and depth of sharing in group meetings should increase during this stage. Self-evaluation, and requests for group feedback, should now focus in part on their progress toward achieving their contract goals.

As in the first stage, parents will complete specific journaling activities and required readings assigned by FLC staff. They will also complete an appropriate physical challenge, such as the ropes course, which they specified in the personal contract. Finally, they will assume minor leadership roles, such as serving as secretary or treasurer of their regional group or assisting in school functions or fund-raising drives.

Stage 3: Leadership (Giving Back)

Parents are ready to enter stage 3 when they have succeeded in achieving some of the goals outlined in their personal contracts and have made a commitment to assuming a leadership role in the Hyde program. This stage is analogous to the excellence stage of student growth; it is characterized by the parent pursuing his or her personal best.

During stage 3, parents demonstrate high self-confidence

and exhibit previously avoided risk-taking behaviors. Now they are expected to model responsible and committed behavior (such as following the Brother's Keeper principle) at all Hyde functions.

In stage 3, parents begin to reach out to their local school community in a spirit of giving back. As before, they will continue to participate in all required Hyde functions and to complete journaling and reading exercises. But they will also take on leadership roles in the Family Learning Center and in their regional groups. They are also expected to become mentors to parents who are still in stage 1 of the growth process.

A First Step

Being a Hyde parent is a demanding role, one that requires plenty of soul-searching and risk taking. But once parents weather the initial shock of examining themselves and sharing with others what they find, they become excited by the reality that selfishly working on their own growth is the best way to help their kids!

As Hyde parents begin the process of self-evaluation, their youngsters begin to examine themselves honestly. As Mom and Dad develop the courage to try new things, so does their son or daughter. As they begin to trust the voice of their own consciences, their children learn to listen to their own inner voices. In addition, as parents grow, they cannot help but forge a deeper bond with their children. A father writes:

> At my Hyde retreat I wrote my first paper. It was about my father and expressed some very deep feelings I didn't know I had.
>
> I terribly miss not having a father. The last time I ever saw him he gave me an Indian Head nickel. As he drove away, I yelled, "I love you, Dad." I saw him only once more before he died. I kept that Indian Head nickel for years.
>
> I shared my paper with my son. As I read it, he cried. Later we both started crying and he said, "Dad, I don't really know you any better than you knew your

Dad. If you died tomorrow, I could only say you were a good provider."

At that very moment I realized I wanted more for both of us and to become a Dad who truly loved him. He said he wanted to share his life with me too. We laughed and cried and agreed we both had to change. It was a first step.

CHAPTER 8

A Call
to Revolution

*Over the years, the ability to look at myself
and the courage to ask difficult questions
have been the real fruits of my Hyde
education.*

—A Hyde alumnus

As I begin this chapter, my thoughts return to graduation morning several years ago. I awake at 5:30 A.M., as I do every graduation day. My speech never comes together until the last moment. Our intensive evaluation process continues up to the evening before the ceremony. My conscience apparently waits until then to begin formulating what I am going to say, then wakes me in time to put it all together.

As I sit at my desk, gazing out the window as the sun peeks over the horizon, I reflect on the events of the past week. My thoughts begin to take order and the basic theme and focus of my speech emerge. I jot down notes to help me retain the thread.

At 9:45 I leave the house, where John Hyde lived before finishing the Hyde Mansion in 1914. I cross High Street and pass through the gates of Hyde, an opening in the massive brick and iron fence that guards the expansive front yard of the Mansion grounds.

As I pass the umbrella tree, the Mansion is still hidden from view by the majestic elms that line the front of the building. Beyond the curved driveway I can see the lily pads on the duck pond, and the stone bridge that joins the island in the middle of the pond to the Mansion grounds. The seniors are beginning to gather on the bridge for the traditional procession to the sunken garden in the rear of the Mansion, where the graduation ceremony will be held.

As I walk up the circular approach to the front portico, the majestic pillars of the Mansion come into view. I stop and look back at the rolling lawn, the gentle movement of the trees, the shadows stretched across the grass as the sun rises above the town.

I hear the metallic clank from the Bath Iron Works below, a continual reminder of the shipbuilding roots of our town. There is also the muted hum of traffic on High Street and the sound of animated conversation coming from the bridge, but somehow the noise doesn't penetrate the peaceful solitude that envelops the Mansion grounds. There is a spiritual quality to this place that time has not diminished.

As I enter the front door of the Mansion, my eye catches the alignment of the three silver chandeliers down the hallway and the four pillars marking the dual stairways rising to the second floor. At the reception desk I look through the glass doors on the right to see if Malcolm is in; the headmaster's office is his now.

The glass doors on the left open to the living room, where countless faculty-student seminars have prepared seniors for the true "commencement" of their lives. I turn down the east-west hallway to my secretary's office for last-minute details or instructions. I return out the north entrance and stroll down the walkway past the parking lot, to the island. All the seniors and faculty are now gathered on the bridge.

In their flowing gowns and formal suits, the graduates look as though they are dressed for a prom. The clear freshness of those faces, the excitement in those eyes, is a spiritually beautiful sight to me. Graduation is a pure moment in the lives of these young men and women. Knowing I am part of the process that brought them here gives me a tremendous feeling of serenity and fulfillment.

There is nervous bantering among the students as we line up for the graduation procession. At 10:00 we begin to "commence," walking by twos until we reach the rear of the Mansion. Its three tiers of patios, latticework, and flower gardens are separated by rounded brick walls that give it the appearance of a fortress. We form two serpentine lines and descend the stairways that grace each side of the sunken garden.

The audience rises and then applauds as the seniors and faculty line up along the Hyde captain's chairs in the front rows of the audience. We all sit down together; graduation has begun.

During the next two hours, every graduate will solemnly walk to the podium and deliver a speech. It is amazing how, in just a few minutes each, the students deeply convey the struggles they've faced and the growth they've achieved during their brief time at Hyde. Some are frank in their assessment of weaknesses still to be overcome. Others express their determination to achieve ambitious goals. Many are unable to control their emotions as they tell their parents how much they love them.

The parents and other family members stand throughout their graduate's entire speech. I am deeply moved by the pride and serenity in their faces as they hear the honesty and conviction in their son's or daughter's voice. As I recall the parent's own struggles in the Family Learning Center, I am reminded of Kahlil Gibran's words that parents "are the bows from which your children as living arrows are sent forth."

As each senior speaks, I can see naked emotions in the tear-stained faces of the faculty. Their toughness has no place here. They have given fully of themselves to their students, and the students are now affirming the power of their spiritual teaching.

It deeply moves me to hear how graduates have been influenced by former students who later joined the Hyde faculty. One of the seniors thanks Ken Grant, who returned to Hyde in 1985 and whose strong commitment to conscience has made him an influential role model for students. I have to smile as I think back to how I started Ken on this road, by directing him as a student to go out and break the Hyde ethics.

Ken later reflected on his own graduation day, and how the Hyde experience has influenced the direction of his life:

> My Hyde graduation was far more a sincere declaration about my future life than just a "graduation." It meant even more than the standard of excellence represented by my Hyde diploma. It symbolized that I was ready to trust my own ethical compass and to accept that my ultimate purpose transcended my own personal ambitions and desires.

Clearly my Hyde education had unearthed a guiding spirit within me, grown stronger with time. . . .

I recently pulled out my 1972 Hyde yearbook, and my eyes fell to a quote by Julian Huxley: "There are two ways of living; a man may be casual and simply exist, or constructively and deliberately try to do something . . . not only about one's own life, but about that of society, and the future possibilities of mankind." I was taken aback by how much I still honor those words, perhaps more passionately than ever.

Establishing a National Model

In 1989, after spending more than two decades refining the unique-potential curriculum at Hyde School, I turned over the reins of leadership to my son, Malcolm, and established the Hyde Foundation, with the goal of helping other schools throughout the country develop educational programs based on the Hyde model. Will Hyde's concept of education work outside the greenhouse conditions of a small prep school in Maine? We'll soon find out: The first Hyde public school program opened in September 1992 in Gardiner, Maine, a blue-collar community with a school system of 2,800 students. A Hyde public school–community model has also been approved in Washington, D.C. Similar models are now on the drawing board in several other major cities.

The 120 families participating in the Gardiner program responded enthusiastically to our intense, week-long summer orientation. "I did things I never thought I could or would do!" one parent remarked. Another added, "My son and I saw each other taking risks, and we developed more respect for each other." A third parent reflected, "I really didn't know my daughter as well as I thought. . . . I feel like I have a brand new family!"

Students were equally excited about what they discovered during the summer session. One student noted, "I got very close to the other students. I feel like I can trust every one of them now. This feeling is so awesome." Another offered, "[I learned] to trust in myself, my thoughts, my feelings . . . to go for or say what I really believe." Still another commented, "I really let loose and had fun. That is something I don't usually do in front of a lot of people."

The powerful learning that occurred during the Gardiner orientation confirms my opinion that our current public school system is tapping less than 20 percent of the potential of parents, students, and teachers. Most of all, it reaffirms my belief that the time is ripe for a bold new approach to education.

Prescription for American Education

We endlessly try to reform America's educational system, with little or no success. We appoint blue-ribbon committees to study our problems. Their conclusions are always dire, their recommendations always the same: beef up academic standards, introduce tougher courses, lengthen the school day or school year, strengthen teacher testing, improve facilities. We implement the reforms, wait a few years, find out they don't work, wring our hands, then begin the reform cycle once again.

If we truly want to transform our educational system, we must put an end to this cycle of ineffective, piecemeal reform and recommit ourselves to the principles on which America was founded and that have successfully guided the Hyde experiment for nearly thirty years: We must reaffirm our belief in the worth and dignity of every individual. We must renew our national commitment to the proposition that all people are created equal. We must resurrect the pioneering, risk-taking, can-do spirit that built America and made it a great nation.

If we want to transform American schools, our first imperative must be to communicate the following convictions to all American kids:

- that they have an important purpose on this earth and the unique potential to fulfill it
- that their true worth is measured, not by their social status, intellect, or talents, but by the strength of their character

- that we admire their attitude and effort, and care less about their actual achievements, because these will come with time if they develop character traits like those emblazoned on the Hyde School shield: Courage, Integrity, Concern, Curiosity, and Leadership.

The wholehearted commitment of parents and schools to the character–unique potential concept will reach the deeper spirit in American youngsters. It will elevate their sights, make them eager to test themselves with difficult challenges, and motivate them to pursue excellence. It will strengthen their self-confidence and bring out their natural desire to contribute.

This commitment to character and unique potential will produce stronger, more confident, more enthusiastic, and capable kids (surely a better way to compete in the global economy than by focusing on higher test scores, master teachers, or longer school hours). In addition, the Hyde approach will have a profound impact on our communities, by drawing out the highest potential of our families, our businesses, and other community institutions and by creating a powerful synergy out of their individual efforts.

The Hyde approach will finally provide what has eluded American education for so long: equality *and* excellence. By focusing on personal criteria of excellence rather than uniform standards of achievement, schools will ensure that every child has an equal opportunity to succeed, regardless of innate abilities or cultural or ethnic background. (This is particularly vital in a society as diverse as the United States.) And when schools begin to concentrate on character development, academic excellence will naturally follow, just as it has at Hyde.

The Hyde approach can be adopted by any school, regardless of economic circumstances. Today money is strongly tied to educational opportunity in America, but it doesn't have to be. A primary reason that private schools are generally superior to public schools is that they are composed of communities of families who care so much about education, they are willing to pay extra for it.

But there's no *need* to pay extra for excellence; wealth is not required to make the Hyde approach succeed. Excellence is rooted in the wholehearted commitment of students; teachers; and, most important, parents. The goal of excellence may appear unattainable to those who live in one of the many depressed areas of America, but the goal *is* within their reach. The first step is to commit to the *idea* of excellence, which will put the American spirit into action—and history has shown the incredible power of that spirit.

Family: The Critical Success Factor

Parents are the critical factor in the success of the Hyde formula. If there is one thing I have learned in my forty-two years of teaching, it is this: to transform American schools, we must transform the typical American family.

Our schools are wasting huge amounts of time and money pursuing the illusion that they can somehow change kids without changing their parents. As long as we allow parents to avoid their own problems and to raise their children as poorly as they damn well please, while we continue to support them educationally, our public schools will never be able to challenge the unique potential of every American kid.

But if we begin to hold families accountable rather than forcing our schools to grapple with family problems, wonderful solutions to our educational woes will begin to appear. And the most powerful pressure for accountability will come, not from the school, but from other families who are committed to giving their children the best possible education.

Let me illustrate: Some years ago we introduced the Hyde concept in a summer program for 150 local elementary school kids. Our success led many parents to attend my first parent-teacher meeting, but I could feel a definite on-guard attitude in the room. As mostly working-class people, these parents weren't comfortable with educators, and I'm sure they had heard some pretty weird things about me besides.

Shortly after the meeting began, one father stood up and made some outlandish comments, criticizing the program before he'd even learned any of the details about it and in spite of the fact that our results were already encouraging. He was clearly finding fault just for the sake of finding fault.

While I silently noted that his son was having similar attitude problems in the program, not one parent said a thing in response. But as the parents began to warm up to me (afterward, one parent remarked, "You're just like me") they relaxed, and the meeting evolved into an honest and open exchange.

Near the end of the meeting, the same father stood up and made another ridiculous comment. But this time the parents spontaneously laughed, and the red-faced man sat down. This was another confirmation of the power of the Brother's Keeper concept: when people share a commitment to achieving their best, they will hold others accountable for doing the same.

But though we must hold parents accountable, we shouldn't expect them to solve their problems alone. Our schools must learn how to assist parents in the difficult process of raising their children, as we do at Hyde. Schools must serve, not just as teaching institutions, but as community centers to which families can turn for support, just as Hyde parents turn to our Family Learning Center when they need help and advice. With family problems and student motivation effectively addressed by parents, the school can guide the entire family and ensure that all their hard work and sacrifice bears fruit.

"Inch by Painful Inch"

If the vision of American education outlined in these pages seems naive, it is only because our present system has brainwashed us into a drastically limited view of what is possible. We defeated Hitler and Japanese imperialism in four years and then sent men to the moon and back in eight. By comparison, our feeble educational reform efforts are pathetic.

Some years ago, when America was experiencing one of its periodic crises of conscience about the sad state of education, a major magazine cover story on the subject concluded that progress in our schools would come "inch by painful inch." As I read that article, my mind returned to a scene at the beach when I was thirteen. After a storm and the most enormous surf I had ever seen, a girl on an innertube was somehow sucked out beyond the surf and was in serious trouble. There was no boat around, so about twenty of us were fighting the huge waves, trying desperately to reach her.

The situation seemed hopeless because our progress was "inch by painful inch." But suddenly I saw a swimmer out beyond the surf. It immediately dawned on me that he'd gone down to the tidal river, had gotten beyond the surf line, and had then swum the entire length of the beach to reach the drowning girl. While we had obviously chosen what had assured our own protection first, then assumed we were doing our best, he had committed himself to saving the girl and then found a solution that would work.

In our hearts, we know we will never solve our educational problems "inch by painful inch." The American spirit demands a truly bold solution—not reform but *revolution*. All it takes is a committed minority to lead the charge.

A Call to Revolution

Most of the American colonists disliked the British monarchy, but it was the only form of governance they had ever known, so the majority of them embraced the status quo. Many of the colonists denounced the Boston Tea Party as an act of lawless renegades. Even after the bloodshed at Lexington and Concord, most colonials still hoped to gain justice by appealing to King George's better instincts.

But in January 1776 Thomas Paine published *Common Sense* to urge the American colonists to fight for the right to become self-governing. Paine's words had a far-reaching impact: half the colonists either read *Common Sense* or heard it read aloud.

In the end, each colonist was forced to choose: either sail back to England or trust in the bold new vision of independence. Though 30 percent of the colonists chose "custom and the crown" and another 40 percent remained uninvolved, the minority who committed themselves to the cause of independence fomented a revolution that resulted in the creation of the United States of America.

Just as a determined minority sparked the American Revolution, so can a committed core of parents, students, and teachers who believe in the unique-potential philosophy ignite a revolution in our schools.

The obstacles will be formidable. Many teachers, administrators, and parents, well entrenched in the present system, will resist the serious changes (including personal changes) required to realize the Hyde vision of education. But such opposition by the old guard, which is inevitable, cannot halt the revolution. As one Gardiner parent writes, the Hyde program "is a process of individual, family, and community growth that, once started, may falter but cannot stop or be stopped."

So if you see the need for a radical change in America's educational system, know that it is only a matter of time before this new revolution occurs. Take heart from the opening words of Thomas Paine's introduction to *Common Sense:*

> Perhaps the sentiments contained in the following pages are not yet sufficiently fashionable to procure them general favor; a long habit of not thinking a thing wrong gives it a superficial appearance of being right, and raises at first a formidable outcry in defense of custom. But the tumult soon subsides. Time makes more converts than reason.

We can continue to cry out "in defense of custom" and leave our educational crisis for the next generation to resolve. Or we can begin to revolutionize our educational system today, and pass on to our children a legacy of which we, and they, can be proud. The truth can't be held back forever. Revolutionary change *will* come to American education; the only question is, When?

Epilogue

After an enthusiastic summer orientation on the Bath campus, the Hyde Foundation's pilot program in Gardiner, Maine, made a promising start when school opened. Then the conflicts between two radically different learning cultures began to surface. Six of the nine teachers in the program quit. I was accused of "bullying" teachers and of trying to "manipulate" the community; those helping me were accused of "disdaining" teachers and of being "liars." Several signs appeared on lawns: "Honk if you hate Hyde"; "Don't drink the Kool-Aid." Finally, in November, the Gardiner-Hyde program was suspended by the Gardiner school board.

A professional mediator was assigned to try to resolve the conflicts between the Gardiner system and Hyde. We tried to modify those aspects of the program that seemed to threaten the teachers. But after twenty-five hours of negotiating with both sides, the mediator declared that mediation was impossible, blaming "teachers' refusal to compromise and a struggle for control in the Gardiner area school district," according to the *Portland Press Herald*.

The ironic truth is that, throughout the controversy surrounding the Hyde program, the vast majority of the Gardiner community, including most of the teachers, agreed that the program is great for kids. It is sad to reflect that the best interests of students were a distant second to the entrenched interests of the Gardiner school district. But it was inspiring to watch the Gardiner-Hyde students and parents fight to save the program. After two months of indecision, the school board finally voted to reinstate the program, by a close five-to-seven vote.

Don't assume Gardiner is an anomaly, some backwoods Maine community that is resistant to change. The same problems that forced the suspension of the Gardiner-Hyde program would have eventually surfaced in any other American school-community—including yours. The previous year we had developed a similar promising program for the Springfield, Massachusetts, school system, receiving 650 preliminary applications for eighth- and ninth-grade families for just 150 places. But at the last moment the local teachers' union voted to postpone the program a year, which effectively killed it. The union's stated reason was that they already had "too much on [their] plate" with their own contract negotiations with the school board.

In the early 1960s many Americans smugly attributed the racial problems in Selma, Alabama, and other Deep South communities to backward "rednecks." The truth is, all white Americans had been indoctrinated into a system that routinely treated blacks as second-class citizens. Now, unfortunately, Americans are still accustomed to an education system that treats children as second-class citizens. It is convenient for people to blame our difficulties in Gardiner and Springfield on the teachers' unions and other vested interests. But we Americans have been immersed in "me-ism" for too many years and have long since forgotten the deeper needs of growing children—if we *ever* understood them. As Pogo said, "We have met the enemy, and he is us."

Our national self-centeredness has generated schools from which everyone takes—and to which few give back. The kids grow up, parents develop other interests, school board members change, and taxpayers focus on shrinking dollars; and this passing parade leaves teachers alone to cope with the children, in schools lacking either a philosophy or a conscience. So the teachers band together into unions, and the unions know that if they stonewall the continual flurry of people's pet reforms, they will survive just by continuing to be there.

We are a nation whose families and teachers are steeped

in a powerful heritage of getting tough jobs done, richly earned by the spirit and sacrifice associated with places like Valley Forge, Gettysburg, and Iwo Jima. Yet we have created schools in which our children cannot find the American dream, in which our teachers find they have to protect themselves, and from which our parents find themselves completely isolated. This was our doing; it is ours to undo. The American spirit, not politicians, educators, and other authorities, will lead us to the right and honorable solution. Obviously I believe the solution will begin once we put character first in our schools. But as this book shows, that won't happen without a fight.

We Americans had to fight ourselves as well as the British to gain our independence. We had to fight ourselves as well as the Confederacy to free the slaves. Now we will have to fight ourselves as well as our education system to free our children.

About the Author

Joseph W. Gauld founded Hyde School in 1966 and served as its first headmaster. Born in Springfield, Massachusetts, he is an economics graduate of Bowdoin College and holds a master's degree in mathematics from Boston University. Gauld had an established career as an educator before breaking away from the traditional system to put his character-first philosophy into action at Hyde. He has now moved on to the Hyde Foundation, which he started in 1989, and works to establish public school models based on the Hyde concept. He still maintains close touch with administrators, faculty, parents, and students at the school he loves.